Author Edmond de Goncourt

Adaptation of the full text

Paris

Copyright Grégori Coudert

ISBN : 9781690153672

EDMOND DE GONCOURT

Outamaro

THE PAINTER OF GREEN HOUSES

Japanese art in the 18th century

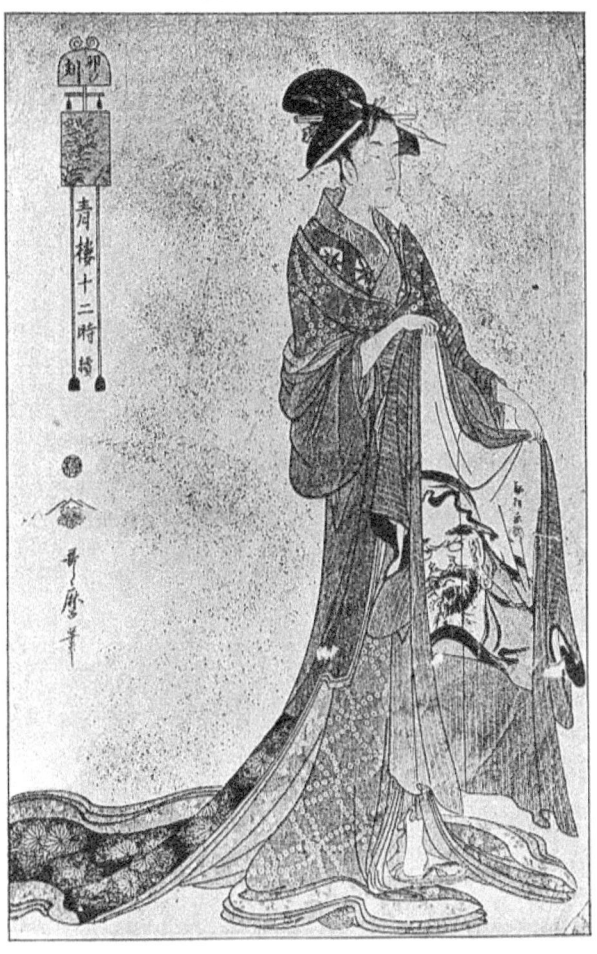

A SHORTER by Outamaro.

Outamaro

THE PAINTER OF GREEN HOUSES

JAPANESE ART IN THE 18th CENTURY

AFTERWORD BY M. J.-H. ROSNY JEUNE

FINAL EDITION

Published under the direction of the Académie Goncourt

PREFACE

In this month, as I enter my seventieth year[1], I am publishing the first volume of a truly intimidating series, because it requires investigations and complicated work in the home: a series that I do not pretend - let it be well known - to bring to a close.

But there is such a charm to work in *new things,* on beings and objects, where you do not meet in front of you, one, two, three, and even ten precursors! It was so interesting for me to make the history of the mores of the Revolution and the Directory, before anyone else! It has been so interesting to make the intimate story of women and things of the eighteenth century, almost as much as anyone else, that my taste for the new, the undeflowered, leads me, as old as I am, to try, for the human century I love, and who is human among the peoples of both hemispheres, to attempt the history of Japanese art, under more or less the same conditions of virginity of the documents in which I wrote the *moral* and artistic history of the Eighteenth Century and the Revolution in France.

Now, no matter where death interrupts this story, I will have on the back of the cover of my first volume, by this simple list of five painters, two lacquerers,

---

[1] This is the year in which the happy Japanese painter, Hokusai, could say: "That he was dissatisfied with everything he had produced until then, and that it was only three years later, that he had more or less understood the shape and true nature of birds, fish, plants, etc., etc., etc. ».

an iron carver, a wooden sculptor, an ivory sculptor, of a bronze-maker[2], an embroiderer, a potter, I would have indicated the means and the method of telling the West, in its various and multiple manifestations, the art of Japan, the only country on earth where industrial art almost always touches the great Art.

This May 26th (day of my birth) 1891.

EDMOND DE GONCOURT.

---

[2] The name of the bronze-maker SEIMIN was forgotten on the cover

Outamaro

I

The Japanese painter, with the family name Kitagawa; the intimate
name Yousouké; the names of the workshop students, first Nobou-
Yoshi, then Mourasakiya[3] ; - it is a habit of Japanese artists to give up
their family name to take a fancy name - finally as the name of a painter
coming out of the studio, and working according to his own inspiration,
the name OUTAMARO was born, According to recent research, in
1754, in Kawagoyé, in the province of Mousashi, and not in Yédo, as
the *Oukiyo-yé Rouikô* says, Kiôden's manuscript work, successively
completed by Samba, Moumeiô, Guekkin, Kiôzan, Tanéhiko, etc. - the
only biography of Japanese painters, of the Oukiyo school, from
Moronobou, not yet printed, but copies of which are shared between
Japanese collectors.

---

[3] Mourasakiya means *purple house, which is the* name of Outamaro's workshop. He did not sign
this name on the prints, but he always kept it in his private life.

Outamaro came to Yédo at a very young age. After a few years of living in unknown homes, he lived with Tsutaya Jûzabro, the famous publisher of illustrated books of the time, whose brand representing a Virginia creeper leaf surmounted by the summit of Fuzi-yama, can be seen on the most perfect impressions of Outamaro, - and who then lived outside the great gate of Yoshiwara.

When Tsutaya Jûzabro moved, and established his shop in Tôri-Àbratchô, in the center of the city, Outamaro followed him there, and lived with him until about 1797, when the publisher died. Then Outamaro successively lived in Kiûyemon-tcbôrue[4] Bakro-tchô street, then settled, in the years before his death, near the Benkei bridge.

First Outamaro studied painting at Kano's school, then became a student of Torima Sekiyen, who seems to have had a very small influence on his talent, according to the sight of his *Hiakkiya ghio,* the Hundred Monsters of the Night and according to the album named after him, where the woman is Koriusai's wife, Shunshô, Harunobou, and is not at all the woman, that Outamaro's wife will be[5].

---

[4] This change of residence, in 1797, made the artist's biographers take this date for the date of his death.

[5] In all of Outamaro's work, I find only one plate that seems to come down from Sekiyen's Chinese *style*: it is a landscape, printed in imitation Chinese ink, part of the six plates of the poetry collection, entitled: The Silver Nature (Snow).

The true inspirers of the way, of the style of Outamaro, are Shighemasa and Kiyonaga, Kiyonaga especially, who endowed Outamaro's talent, even becoming the personal founder of the school of which he is the head and teacher, with a little of the graceful lengthening of the oval of his female figures, a little of the soft flexibility of his sizes, a little of the voluptuous undulation of the fabrics around the bodies.

This appropriation of Kiyonaga's drawing is obvious in these two plates representing a tea house by the sea, where a woman brings her top dress, her black dress with armor, to a Japanese lord taking a cup of tea; a composition, which, if it were not signed Outamaro, would be taken by any Japanese collector, for a Kiyonaga, a composition that Mr. Hayashi believes that she was executed in Kiyonaga's studio, around 1770, but certainly not after 1775, and at a time when the painter was barely twenty years old, if he had them.

She is also sensitive to this appropriation in the beautiful impression showing this great woman, with her dress sown with cherry blossoms on a red background, and to whom a wrestling doll is brought, and which, still according to Mr. Hayashi's feeling, was published before 1775.

There is even finally this appropriation, in the six admirable *guesha* boards celebrating the *Niwaka, the* Yoshiwara Carnival, the first edition of which would be 1775, and where the boards, while belonging a little more to Outamaro, are signed in a powerful style, a little Junonian style, if you can say, given to his wives by the master, who preceded the painter of the Green Houses by at least twenty years in his life, but where Outamaro- still borrows details from Kiyonaga, such as the one of these pretty heart-warmers disheveled around the temples and cheeks, bringing such a loving character to the figures.

The first knowledge that the Japanese public had of Outamaro's talent was in the illustration of popular novels, in the illustration of these small-format books, with yellow covers, black prints, common paper, a little bit of devil printing, and which are called, in Japan, *Kibiôshi*, Yellow Books, taking their name from the color of their covers: - publications!! cheap, and of a great sale, on which the artist worked from the day of his debut, in 1783, until 1790.

Of these little five-cent books, I have a copy on hand: it is the story of the Aoto "sapèque" (qian, Chinese coin), by Kioden Kitao Masayoshi. Aoto-ga-Zeni, a former well-known judge, lost a "sapèque" in a river one day and had the idea of hiring men to find it, which cost him a hundred times more than the small coin he had lost. After that, he says:

"What is *paid to men is not lost, but what is left in the river is not of interest.* "In this little book, there is already a spiritual rendering of women's attitudes and movements of grace, and in a composition representing a struggle between men and women, the artist is beginning to show a certain knowledge of anatomical forms.

The success of these small books printed in black led publishers to launch series of a larger format, more carefully executed, and where, every year, Outamaro's talent grew. These are: The Bouquet of the Word, 1787; The Sparrows of Yedo, 1788, The Different Classes of the Japanese Population, 1780; The Dance of Surugha. 1790, etc., etc.

In 1785, two students trained by Outamaro began, as did his help in the illustration of the Yellow Books, Mitimaro and Yukimaro.

At the beginning, Outamaro stood out for its originality. It was the habit of the artists of that time to make their popularity a little bit with the popularity of the actors they represented, and in this country, where the elderly, the young, the men, the women were and are still fanatical theatrical celebrities, to take advantage, for their name, of the fashion of such or such. Outamaro refused to draw actors, proudly saying: "*I don't want to shine in favor of the actors, I want to found a school that owes nothing but to the talent of the painter*".

And when, in Ohan-Tchôyémon's play, the actor Itikawa Yaozô had an immense success, and that his portrait drawn by Toyo-kouni, obtained a considerable flow, he, Outamaro, represented the play, but only represented by elegant women, playing6 in imaginary compositions, thus demonstrating in this series of images that the draughts men of the vulgar school, who had repeated this subject, in Toyokouni's way, were a troupe emerging from their workshops, a troupe comparable to *ants, coming out of rotten wood.*

V

---

[6]Despite his haughty disregard for the compositions of his colleagues, representing theatre scenes, I do not know if Outamaro drew several of them hîmself, but I can assure you that he did draw one, which I have before me. It is a long sourimono of a much larger format than usual, featuring a Japanese drama, in which seventeen actors are gathered.

After the *Kibiôshi,* the Yellow Books, printed in black, Outamaro approaches the color image, clans of large-format polychrome engravings, in the *Nishiki-yé* (*nishiki,* brocade, silk with artistic drawings, and *yé,* painting, drawing, image): polychrome engravings, where, according to his biographers, Outamaro reaches "the sublime of beauty and luxury".

These wonderful impressions begin by being compositions of two, three, five, six, seven leaves.

In the impressions composed of seven leaves, which are not numerous, let us mention: Procession of the Korean ambassador, reproduced in a Niwaka (carnival) by *guesha* (singers and dancers).

An endless parade of women on foot and on horseback, escorting one of their own, in a litter box resembling a chestnut: all these women wearing strange pointed green hats and dressed in harmonious dresses, where blue, green, purple and yellow remind us of the decoration of the Chinese porcelains of the green family, colors that had such a great influence on the Japanese masters' watercolors, prior to Outamaro.

In the series of prints composed of five sheets, let us quote:

Boys' Day

A woman leaning over an album, next to another woman, with a brush in her hand, getting ready to paint: both looked at by a child in a room, where on a rotating easel crowned with a small parasol, is fixed a kakemono representing, in a red, blood color, the terrible Shôki, the exterminator of the devils, a kind of boss of boys.

And let us give here, according to Mr. Anderson, the legend of this devil exterminator: Chung Kwei, the devil hunter, one of the favorite myths of the Chinese, was considered to be a supernatural protector of Emperor Ming Hwang (713-762 AD) against the evil spirits that haunted his palace. His story is told in the *E-honko-jidan*: Emperor

Genso was once caught with a fever, and in his delirium, he saw a little demon stealing his mistress Yokiki's flute *(Yang-Kwei-fei); at the* same time a strong spirit appeared, seized the demon, and ate it. When the Emperor asked him his name, he replied: "I am Shinshi Shôki, from Shunan Mountain. During the reign of Emperor Koso (Kao-Tsu) in the Butoku period (618-627 CE), I could not achieve the rank I aspired to in the higher positions of the state, and out of shame I killed myself. But at my funeral, I was elevated, by imperial order, to posthumous dignity, and now I seek to recognize the favor granted to me. That's why I want to exterminate all the demons on earth. »

Genso woke up and found that his illness had disappeared. He then gave Godoshi the order to paint the devil's exterminator, and to distribute copies throughout the Empire.

THE NEW YEAR'S DAY MARKET

The Market takes place during the last ten days of the year and is held in front of the main gate of the Assa-Kousa temple. A crowd walking in the middle of mountains of buckets, sieves, household utensils, and which is overcome here and there, carried on a head, by a New Year's gift, especially in Japan: a lobster on a fern bed, a straw tortilla to drive the devils out of the houses, etc. In the most hurried of the crowd, where two little girls, in order not to get lost, hold each other by a piece of cloth held tightly in their hands, a boy raises a small pagoda, a toy pagoda, at the end of his arms, in the air for sale.

THE STORM

A torrential rain, drowning, sabotaging the landscape.

A young girl plugging her ears to the sound of distant thunder. A crying child reaching out his little arms to his mother, so that she could take him on herself. Everywhere umbrellas that open in a hurry. And in the middle board a loving couple, running under the same umbrella, the woman in the pretty slenderness of the Atalante in the Tuileries garden; the couple joined and followed closely by a friend, nestled in the speed of the trio.

I don't know of any image that gives a more real, more conspicuous representation, clinging more or less in the air to the legs of people running in a panic.

THE GREAT CLEANING OF A GREEN HOUSE AT THE END OF THE YEAR

The maidservants, washing in the morning, cleaning the house thoroughly, which takes place around the last days of December, and in the boulevard of furniture and screens knocked over to the ground, scaring away small groups of mice with brooms, feathers, water from the leaching, with the brushes.

In my first work, I had believed this impression composed of only three impressions, because it is the state where it is usually found, but it has five.

The fourth board shows a woman lifting under her arms to put him on her feet, a sleepy young Japanese man, whom it is time to put on the door, and whose cowardly hand is trying to attach his sword to his belt.

The fifth board represents the awakening of an old man, so funny in his contortions and ridiculous stretching, that a woman runs away laughing.

As for the compositions of three Outamaro leaves, these triptych images, particularly fond of Japanese artists, are innumerable.

Let's mention a few of them in the most different genres:

An interior, where a lottery is drawn by means of a rather original riddle. A woman presents a twisted strand, with the ends untied, and the prize is won by the one who chooses the twine strand, to which the prize is attached. In the end, a woman brings a lot to replace the lot being pulled.

THE WEDDING

The daimio and the noble woman are sitting opposite each other. The bride has in front of her the three bowls, in which she must drink three times: this number three having a meaning, because multiplied it makes the number nine, considered there as the most productive number in the multiplication of species.

And while in the end a woman takes the two bottles of sake offered to the *kami,* spirits, a woman, next to the bride, has on a plate a dry fish, which is not eaten, but is superstitiously served as good luck to the bride and groom, another woman brings soup in bowls of lacquer with gold drawings, another woman heats the sake in a long-handled teapot, called *tchôshi*[7].

---

[7] Here is the description of the marriage, given by Hayashi; in the issue on Japan, published by Gillot.

The engagement gift consists of two silk dresses, white and red, three barrels of sake, three fishes; but in the poor class, this gift is reduced to a cotton dress.

The dowry does not exist, but the bride brings enough to set up her household, in clothes, furniture, objects for daily use, and in a rich marriage, these objects that we carry constitute a real procession.

The wedding ceremony consists of completing the *Sakadzuki* formality (special sake cups). The main lounge is the chosen place. The fiancée first takes the place of the mistress of the house, the alleged one sits in the place of the main guest, in ordinary cases. The man wears the official costume and the woman the white dress. Parents and friends take their seats in the order indicated.

In a palace, with a succession of updated buildings in the middle of gardens, showing the characters in these light aerial perspectives of the country, a dancer in a red dress, dances, a flower hat on her head, a flower hat at the end of each hand, admirably looked at by the leading women, and at the back, at the very back, by the daimio and his friends.

In the board on the right, she is a woman lying on the ground in a pose of sad collapse, and as if ready to faint, near a letter that fell beside her.

In the left plate, it is the literary painter Kioden-Masayoshi, - yes, the painter himself bearing his name on his sleeve - fanning himself with a fan, where it is written: *It is good for a poet to be a clumsy, because if his verses had the talent to shake the sky and the earth, he would really be very unhappy! It is* on this fan, a *Kioka,* a small light poetry, a small ironic poetry, mocking a lyrical poetry of the seventh century, affirming that the true poet has the power to *make his verses tremble in heaven and earth.*

About this fan, about the fan decorated with gold leaves, either with bird and flower paintings or with *kioka,* - about the fan of such general use among all Japanese of all sexes, and at all times of life, let us say that the best, most artistic, are made in Kiolo, and let us tell the strange

---

The ceremony is presided over by a lady of honor among the healers or by an intermediary among the people. Three sake cups are carried in front of the man, placed on a special display case. The man first takes the first cup, and drinks three different times. Then he begins the second cut that he offers to the woman. She drank there three times, then began the last vial, and offered it to the man who finished it three times. Once this is done, the marriage is concluded.

Then come dinner and celebration.

origin of the fan.

During the reign of Emperor Tenji, around 670, a resident of Tomba, seeing bats bending and spreading their wings, had the idea of making leaf fans, which were not later named *Kuwahori, which* means bat.

There are two species of fans in Japan, one called *Sensu, which* folds, and the other of round shape which does not fold, and which are made with bamboo or *chamœ cyparis obtusa.*

There is a third species of very rich fan, which is used by dancers, either to beat the bar or to develop graceful gestures, called *uchiwa,* and which is sometimes made of silk.

During the Kuwambun period, a priest named Gensei, famous for his artistic taste and poetry, began to make fans of admirable perfection himself in Fukakusa, fans that acquired a great reputation, and which were known as *Fukakusa uchiwa.*

This composition of the dance of a guesha in a daimio palace, where Outamaro stages his colleague Kioden Masayoshi, seems to have been drawn in color, after a drawing of a scene from real life in Japan, which is quite rare in the master's work.

A Japanese prince, holding a basket of shells in his hand, in the middle of salt carriers.

It is the staging of a story or legend of a prince, relegated to exile on an island[8], where he had become the lover of two salt-bearing sisters, whom he had all the trouble to abandon, when he was called and restored in his honors.

The struggle between his loves and what he owed to his rank, gave rise to the most touching scenes in a novel entitled *Matzugazé-*

---

[8] Undoubtedly the island of Fatsisio, a penitentiary island, where princes and courtiers in disgrace were deported and used to make and decorate, according to Mr. Fraissinet, the admirable dresses of the Hague Museum.

Mourasamé: the names of the two fishermen. And the anecdote of love and romance also provided a number of plays.

A harmonious board is the composition representing women, at night, having fun catching fireflies.

There they are, six young women, in their softly visible dresses, in the middle of the chiaroscuro of the pale darkness of a warm August night, there they are, dropping, with screens, the luminous fireflies of the tree branches, putting in this hunt an ingeniously clumsy grace. And we see a little girl venturing, barefoot, into a stream, to grab the glow worms, shining in the reeds, while a little boy and a little girl carry the boxes that serve as their prison, looking curiously inside.

THE CULTURE OF ENGRAVINGS IN YÉDO. THE PRODUCTION OF THIS CITY.

A first plate shows the inside of a shop, with walls covered with kakemonos, a ceiling full of color images suspended on strings, while a fairground merchant has just bought prints, which a woman shows him. The second board, of the greatest rarity, which Mr. Gonse alone owns in Paris, introduces us to the workshop, where a woman cuts the wood with a chisel that she hits with a mallet, where another woman leaning on a table is about to draw the nets of a board, while a third woman, crouched in a corner, sharpens her tools on an ironing stone.

In the third plate, we see in the back room, in these allegorical compositions that the Japanese like, we see Outamaro, under the figure of a woman, submitting to another woman, who would be the personification of the publisher, a drawing to engrave.

PILGRIMAGE TO ISÉ.

In a place famous for its sunrises, in Isé, near these two rocks coming out of the sea, connected by a straw cable, near these sacred rocks, called Miôto-Iwa (rocks of the couple) and considered as the emblem of a husband and a wife, and to whom the newlyweds come to pray for the happiness of their marriage and the birth of children, a society of women on the beach have fun taking off their shoes and walking barefoot in the stream, their long dresses raised with both hands.

WOMEN ON A JOURNEY.

An original composition depicting three women in front of a mosquito net, under which three other women, half visible, half erased behind the lattice, make bedtime preparations, talking with the women in the foreground.

We meet there with one of the usual attempts at the same time as with one of the successes of the artist's brush, to oppose women in full light, women in a green penumbra, women in the state of pretty Chinese shadows behind a paper frame, and Outamaro has such a strong taste for these oppositions, and these beings or parts of beings, shown in the chiaroscuro of the hue of the environments that, in the color impression of the "DYERS", he makes a child lean for a kiss towards the figure of his little sister, curiously purple, in the tone of the large purple band, through which we see his face[9].

YORITOMO'S CRANES.

A meeting of young women, under a pink sky, all lit up by white cranes fluttering in the air, a poem in the paw, and in which a Japanese

---

[9] Very often, Outamaro looks for original painting effects in these reflections putting on people and faces, strange, strange, unexpected shades; this is how a large courtesan's head appears to you, the half-pink figure of the pink veil she holds in front of her, and with on the skin, the seedling of white dots, which make the veil ornament.

woman passes the small strip loaded with writing, to another Japanese woman, holding a crane, to whom she will give freedom.

A composition allegorically reminiscent of an anecdote of the life of Yoritomo[10], who, on the hearsay that storks lived a thousand years old, one day gave a thousand storks a flight, with the day and year of their flight, attached to their legs, and it is claimed in Japan that these storks were found in the sixteenth century.

But among these *triptych images*, perhaps the most sought-after, the rarest of all is that of the DIVERS, *the awabi* fishermen, the shells we eat.

This triple plate happens to be the composition where the nude of the woman[11] is revealed, in the most ostensible way, as understood and made by Japanese painters. It is the woman's nude, with a perfect knowledge of her anatomy, but a simplified nude, summarized in its masses, and presented without details, in lengths a little *mannequined,* and by a line that seems calligraphied.

The leaf on the left depicts a naked woman, the lower part of her

---

[10] The usurper Minamolo Yoritomo, whose advent ended the struggle between the clans of Taira and Minamoto, used it as the first hereditary shogun, a title conferred on him in 1190 AD.

[11] In fact, without going back to another century, we have, without going back to another century, the publication, a few years before, of the colorful plate of the Kiyonaga WOMEN'S BATH where the great artist, precursor of Outamaro, gave us the graceful outline of Games or three naked young women, and the pretty indiscretions of pieces from other bodies, under half-opened bathrobes, and again this pretty lower body of a woman, who, her head and torso masked by a blind, shows only one leg lying on the ground and one leg raised on the step of a platform, and one hand wiping in between the two legs. It's very learned, very real naked, but where I don't find the great style of form and line, characterizing the DIVERS.

body veiled with a flap of red cloth, cast at the edge of the bank, one leg already in the sea, with a shiver in her body leaning on both hands thrown behind her, and with the retraction in the air of a foot that seems to take up twice, to definitely enter the water. Above his head, a second fisherman leaned over, showing him, with his outstretched arm, something in the abyss.

The middle leaf shows us sitting a fisherwoman, a blue cotton pad thrown on her shoulders, combing her hair dripping with water, while a child, naked, heads her upright.

The sheet on the right shows us a fisherwoman, her knife to open the shells in her mouth, and in a graceful circumvention of the torso, twisting with both hands the tip of the wet cloth surrounding her loins, while a buyer, kneeling, chooses a shell from her basket.

These tall, long women, with all-white bodies, scattered black hair, with pieces of red around them, in these pale greenish landscapes, are images of a very great style, having a charm that stops, surprises, amazes[12].

There is another triptych board of the DIVERS.

---

[12] This board, which I paid 40 francs five or six years ago, has just been bought for 1,050 francs at the Burty sale by Mr. Samuel. Besides, it's a very rare board! We only know three proofs in France, at Mr. Gonse's, at Mr. Duret's, at mine, and one proof in America at Boumgarten's, in New York, Hayashi who has her picked up in Japan, has so far been unable to obtain one. For me, I don't think there are two states, I think, which happens quite often in Japanese prints, that without new removal, there are changes in the coloring of the printing of the plates; that's how the woman buying an *awabi* is in a green dress in Burty's proof, and that in my test tube and that of Duret, she has a purple and green dress.

However, it is indisputable that Mr. Gonse's trial, whether of a second or first state, is incomparably more beautiful than Burty's trial.

This composition represents, in a first compartment, two women undressing in a boat; in a second, a diver climbing into a boat, helped by her comrade; in a third, the diver swimming as she dives underwater, - and from the shore, walkers looking at the divers.

In this color impression, the women are smaller, cuter, slimmer and graceful, and with the lean delicacy of their bodies under their thick wet black hair, they have in the water something of the vague fluidity of the hair appearances, under which the Japanese represent the dead souls, returning to the earth.

VI

Then after these great compositions, there are series for albums, of six, seven, ten, twelve, twenty plates, etc., some of which appeared simultaneously with the great compositions, but most of which were performed later.

And in these series, perhaps even better than in the great compositions, the Japanese woman appears, so to speak, in the betrayal of her daily occupations in the house and garden. The Japanese woman appears gilded on her lips; removing the down from her face with the country's razor; making the knot of her belt with both hands, worn behind when she is an honest woman, worn in front when she is a courtesan, - making this knot, sometimes holding with her chin against her neck, some novel illustrated from there; folding silk, a corner of the cloth in her mouth, loving to chew; arranging irises in a cornet: bathing a bird; smoking a silver pipette; adding ivory nails to her fingers to play koto; painting a *kakemono* or *makimono;* writing poems on strips, which she attaches to the first cherry trees in bloom; shooting a bow in a room, with the arrows pricked at her fingertips; hiding her face under the cheeky mask, to Okamé's big laugh[13].

---

[13] This mask with its narrow forehead, its huge jowls, its big hilarity in a hen's ass mouth: this mask attached almost clans in all the vestibules of Japanese houses, like an invitation to good humor on the visitors' backs, is the figuration under which the Japanese represent the goddess Odzoumé who plays this role in this famous Japanese mythological legend.

The powerful goddess, born of the marriage of Isanagni and Izanani, the first two male and female deities, creators of Japan, the Sun goddess, to whom her father had given the command of the sky, who ruled from the top of the column, where she had ascended, was constantly tormented by the wicked mischief of her brother, the god of the Moon, whose Empire was the Blue Sea, and who united by throwing at his head the corpse of a piebald horse, which he had skinned from head to tail: brutality that had given her such a fright that she had injured herself with the shuttle she was currently weaving on. And in her fear, the goddess had withdrawn into a cave, whose entrance she had closed with a massive door, made of a gigantic rock.

Heaven and earth, following this retreat of the goddess, had been plunged into darkness, which the wickedest gods had filled with a hum, which had brought general horror.

It was then that all the gods, assembled in the dry bed of the Amenoyasou River (river of heavenly peace), held a council to appease the goddess, and pulling iron from the celestial mines, the god Itchi Koridomé, assisted by the divine blacksmith Amatsumoré, succeeded in forging a huge and perfect mirror, representing the august deity of Isé.

During the manufacture of this mirror, other gods planted the *Kodzou* (Broussonieta) and basa (hemp), and mixing the bark of the first with the free bark of the second, made clothes for the goddess, and other gods built her a palace, and other gods made her jewelry and shaped her a sacred scepter in sakaki wood.

After pulling a favorable augury from a deer bone, thrown into a cherry wood fool, one of the back gods uprooting a great tree, hung the mirror from it, and began to crow the power and beauty of the princess, in the middle of the *cocorico of* an innumerable gathering of roosters.

And the god Takadjira (with powerful arms), was stationed near the cave door, at the moment when the goddess Oudzoumé, with her hair adorned with moss, her sleeves

And it is not simply on paper that it is remembered, in a spiritual trait, of the woman's occupation, it is in its absolute reality the retracement of nature, of altitude, of poses, of the familiar gesture of that occupation, finally the surprise of the particular mimicry, which characterizes any race of a country, any society at a time. And you have the Japanese woman in all the intimate movements of her body; you have her in her sheet metal supports on the back of her hand, when she reflects, in her kneeling, the palms of her hands resting on her thighs, when she listens, in her speech, thrown aside, her head a little turned, and who shows her in the so beautifully evasive aspects of a lost profile; you have her in her loving contemplation of flowers that she looks at flattened on the ground; you have her in her reversals, where she slightly sits, half seated, on the balustrade of a balcony; you have it in her readings, where she reads in the volume very close to her eyes, both elbows resting on her knees; you have it in her toilet, which she does

---

rolled up with a liana, began to play a bamboo flageolet, accompanied by a god pinching the six strings of six bows, knocked down on the ground, with the rustling of the rods of a rough grass, while the other gods beat the measure with wooden planks.

Then Odzoumé started dancing, singing:

God contemplate the door,

Look at the majesty of the goddess!

The goddess of the Sun, hearing the great praise that was being given to her, said: "In recent times, men have implored me a lot, but nothing so beautiful has ever happened to me. "And pushing the door of her cave slightly, she said again: « I imagined that as a result of my retirement, Japan was plunged into darkness. Why does Oudzoumé dance and why do the gods laugh so hard? »

Oudzoumé replied to the Sun Goddess: "I dance, and they laugh, because there is here a divinity (referring to the suspended mirror), a divinity superior to yours.

As the goddess moved her head a little forward to see him, Takadjira, the god with strong arms, grabbed her by the hand, pulled her out of her cave, and a cord of rice straw placed behind her, prevented her from entering it.

Okamé is the vulgar name of the goddess Oudzoumé.

with one hand holding in front of her, her little metal mirror, while with the other hand passed behind her, she caresses herself distractedly with the neck of her screen; you have it in the circumvention of his hand around a sake cup, in the delicate and curled touch of his monkey fingers, around the lacquers, porcelains, small artistic objects of his country; you finally have him the woman of the Empire of the Sunrise in his languid grace, and in his pretty crawling on the mats of the floor.

Browse through these thousands of images, and at each sheet the kind pictures. Look at these women, in reverie lending themselves to such charming attitudes behind the *shoji*[14]: Look at this young girl sitting in front of a house, sitting from behind on her open hands, one leg raised on the chest that serves as her seat, and the other leg hanging, her foot out of the shoe that fell to the ground; look at this pretty

---

[14] One feature of Japanese housing, says Remy in his NOTES ON JAPAN, is the extent of the openings reserved for it. There are walls only on the side exposed to rain, around the door, in the outbuildings, kitchens, cabinets, etc. These walls made of blackened planks or slats coated with clay and mortar do not go as far as the ground, they are supported by the floor, which is always suspended 50 centimeters from the ground, on posts giving the house the appearance of a piling construction.

There are still large gaping openings between the construction posts, which are closed by movable partitions of two different kinds. Some of them are solid and made of large wooden shutters, which rest on the edge of the floor, and climb up to the roof by sliding into the grooves and remind us of our store closures. They are only used at night, and in anticipation of earthquakes, small doors are reserved for quick escape in case of danger. The other partitions that limit the apartments themselves are placed one meter behind the first ones, so that the floor area left free between them forms a balcony during the day, a corridor at night. This inner wall called *shoji* is a real curiosity of Japan, because of the role that paper plays in it. It is a fir frame supporting a rectangular grid tightened in wooden rods, on which are stretched and glued sheets of white and thin paper, which replace glass - and behind which, let us say, the people who pass take on the character of Chinese shadows, which are reproduced in the images.

musician, followed by her *schamisen* wearer, walking to go home, where she must make music, walking as if with a kind of shy grace, in this dark night, under a sky that seems starry from the snow that falls; Look at these two young girls lying all the way down on the floor, both elbows on the ground, both hands opposite each other, and struggling to get her friend's hand down; look at these two young girls who talk to each other, with one arm around their necks, and whose two free hands join in front of them, in a movement of prayer; look again, always look...

And it is a parade of these elegant women, with their upper body material, their dress wrapped tightly around their loins and thighs, which, according to Geoffroy's happy expression, flattens and gives them "the curve of a sword", a dress whose downward expansion spreads and spins, at their feet, in waves and waves.

VII

Of all these series, the most beautifully telling entitled *Seirô jûnitoki, which* translates into the: TWELVE HOURS OF GREEN HOUSES. Yes, the twelve Japanese hours responding to the twenty-four European hours, yes, the Mouse hour, which is midnight; the Beef hour, which is two hours: the time of the Tiger, which is four o'clock; the time of the Rabbit, which is six o'clock; the time of the Dragon, which is eight o'clock; the time of the Serpent, which is ten o'clock; the time of the Horse, which is noon; the time of the Sheep, which is two o'clock; the time of the Monkey, which is four o'clock; the time of the Rooster, which is six o'clock; the time of the Dog, which is eight o'clock; the time of the Boar, which is ten o'clock: - These twelve Japanese hours,

Outamaro symbolized them in elegant altitudes and charming women's groups.

And never has Outamaro had a more delicate lineage of the woman, in her movements of grace, than in this series, at the same time as the painter of the beautiful dresses of the East, has never shown in these women, as if dressed in the bright colors of the anemone, a more distinguished taste of clothing, and has nowhere made a more original choice of silks, with soft and shimmering colors. Roses, so pink in color that they seem to notice through a tulle, mauves degrading so nicely into a pigeon's throat, greens in a water-green shade, blues, bluish only from the nothing of a cloth turned blue, and a whole series of unspeakable grays, grays that seem tinged with distant, quite distant reflections, of bright colors.

It is because for her dresses, the Japanese woman has a taste for the most distinguished, the most *artistic*, the most distant from the taste that Europe has for clear colors.

The whites that the Japanese woman wants on the silk she wears are: *Aubergine white* (greenish white), *fish belly white* (silver white); roses are: *pink snow* (pale pink), *peach blossom snow (light* pink); blues are: *bluish snow* (light blue), *sky black* (dark blue), *peach blossom moon* (pink blue); yellows are honey color (light yellow), etc. The reds are: jujube red, *flame, smoky* (brown red), *silver ash* (ash red); the greens are: tea green, crab green, shrimp green, *onion heart* green (yellowish green), *lotus shoot green* (yellowish light green)[15]: all broken and charming colors for the eye of the colorist, all colors with adorable shades, said false in our country.

Now if a bride's trousseau, a little well-off in Japan, has twelve ceremonial dresses: a blue dress embroidered with jasmine stems and

---

[15] THE HOUSE OF AN ARTIST, by Edmond do Goncourt. Carpenter, 1881. T. Ier.

bamboos for the first month; a sea green dress with cherry blossoms and checks for the second month; a sparse red dress with willow branches for the third month; a grey dress, where the cuckoo, the bird of good omen, is painted or embroidered for the fourth month; a dull yellow color, covered with iris leaves and aquatic plants, for the fifth month; an orange color, on which watermelons are embroidered, for the sixth month, where the rains and ripening of these melons begin; a white robe, speckled with *kounotis,* purple flowers in bells, whose medical and edible root is assimilated by gourmets to the nests of the Salangan swallow, for the seventh month; a red robe sprinkled with mimosa leaves or Japanese plum tree, for the eighth month; a purple robe, decorated with flowers of the matricaria, for the ninth month; an olive robe, sprinkled with harvest fields, crossed by paths, for the tenth month; .a black robe, embroidered with allusive ice characters, for the eleventh month; a purple robe, filled with ideographic signs expressing the rigors of winter, for the twelfth month, - so if there is, I repeat, as Mr. Fraissinot in her CONTEMPORARY JAPAN, these twelve dresses, one dress per month in the trousseau of a wealthy Japanese woman, what other wardrobe still had a great courtesan, and the luxurious and original dresses that Outamaro painted in the Yoshiwara's cloakroom.

However, Outamaro painted us purple dresses, where, in the pink degradation of the bottom of the dress, birds run on the branches of trees in bloom, purple dresses, through which zigzag, woven in white, the insect characters of the Japanese alphabet, purple dresses, where there are landslides of fierce Korean lions, in old bronze colors; - purple dresses, with a slightly beveled tone, flowered with white irises on their green stems; - blue dresses, of this fresh blue, which China named blue of *the sky after the rain,* under large pink payment peonies; - grey dresses, branches in all directions of twig and whitish bushes, giving them the appearance of dresses painted in grey: - green pea dresses, as if enameled with pink cherry blossoms; green dresses of a colorless water green, disappearing under these paulownia flowers, which are the coat of arms of the ruling family: from flowers to stems. violets, with three large white leaves; - purple dresses, furrowed with rivers, where the lower edge shows the walk of mandarin ducks; - fawn-brown dresses, where clusters of wisteria hang; - black dresses, which make such beautiful repellers in this stallion of colored dresses, black dresses, flowered with chrysanthemums or pine needles, embroidered in white; black dresses, with lanceolate leaves of caladium covered in snow; black dresses or *tay* roses, in baskets of sparterie, are mixed with screens, with command scepters; - dresses, dresses, dresses, dresses, where there are passages of heraldic cranes, lattices imitating cages, where birds fly, Greeks mixed with fans, Dharma heads painted with Indian ink, small bouquets of intertwined hatching, arrangement of dress that Outamaro's drawing likes, and under which he makes the portrait (the beloved women: finally, all the things and beings of the living and inanimate nature, and who deserve to be called dresses-paintings.

Let us not forget the pretty light dresses, where there are reproductions of these diffuse starfish, painted in all colors: these dresses with a white background; this one crossed by vague and unstopped pink bands, with which the Japanese translate on lacquer and fabrics, the purple clouds of the sunset; this one all historized of azure chicks.

And on the colored dresses, Outamaro wears belts with dull tones, belts very often green, yellow designs of old gold, whose tones are related to the tones of old fabrics of the past, and sometimes seek a certain green, called in Japan *Yama bato iro,* color of mountain pigeon, and that only the Mikado had the right to wear once.

And in this country, where the bright tones of clothes are reserved for children, when Outamaro is led to make his dresses rich, this wonderful couturier takes care of them, an art to avoid the blatant glow, the *scoundrel* sight. When he decorates a dark robe with butterflies, instead of brightly colored butterflies, he paints fawn, yellowish butterflies, harmonizing with the background; when he decorates it with peonies, he never chooses them in a single tone, and attenuates their whiteness by a purpurine hue; finally, when he decorates it with arabesques, he manages to kill the snoring of the decoration, by the seriousness of the tone of the arabesques on a neutral background.

And always, always the sobriety in the ornamentation, and these seedlings of predilection on the dresses of some flowers, resembling the petals reported on the fold of a sleeve, on a shoulder, on a walk under flowering trees.

IX

After the TWELVE HOURS OF THE GREEN HOUSES that have nothing (the special property of the "Green Houses" and which represent twelve attitudes of courtesans, at the morning, evening, day and night hours, the series, the most perfect in my opinion, would be the series of six SIGNS OF THE MOST FAMOUS SAKE HOUSES, *depicted by six courtesans;* an original series, each plate of which represents at the top the sake barrel in its envelope of sparterie, on which stands out in black the manufacturer's mark, and surmounted on the left by a branch of flowering shrub, on the right by a red lacquer cup containing an inscription. Below, a little in the arrangement of our heraldic figures at the bottom of a crest, is kneeling or squatting, a beautiful of the Yoshiwara in the year 1790.

I must admit that I do not know, in any country, any impressions of such a deliciously dying harmony, and where the colors seem to be made of what remains of color in the water well where a brush has been washed: colors that are no longer colors, so to speak, but clouds that recall these colors.

And these six women, with their soft colors, are removed from a yellow background, from above a purple mat.

Another beautiful series is the one in which Outamaro interprets the preface to the History of the Ronins, which states: "*a nation where the acts of nobility and courage of the brave samurai would not be published, would be comparable to a dark night, in the darkness of which we would not see a star sparkling*" and popularizes, with the allegorical tendency of his mind to reproduce everything by the grace of the woman, the TWELVE PAINTINGS OF THE FORTY SEVEN RONINS FORMED BY THE MOST BEAUTIFUL WOMEN

Komei-Bijin Mitate Tchûshingura), a series in which, in moving groups and graceful female layers, amidst light fabrics, a woman's black dress stands out with almost dramatic power.

Finally, I will mention THE CHILDREN DRESSED AS SIX POETS. 1790. muted, amortized colors, where the reds a little brick, the yellows a little carnation of India, the mauves a little red, the greens a little olive, have a small kinship with the colors that the Louis XIII tapestries were looking for.

Then afterwards it's: THE SIX POETESSES. - THE SIX BEAUTIFUL FIGURES OF YEDO, *composed at the Six Rivers of the Tamagawa River.* - THE FIVE DAYS OF CELEBRATION - THE LOVERS' LOYALTY CONTEST, etc., etc., etc.

Let us not forget among these sequences of color prints, a second, a third sequence of compositions, inspired by the forty-seven ronins.

Let us not forget either the "Making of silk" or more literally: the

SILKWORM WORKERS, *Joshoku Kaiko Tewazagusa,* a series less than the TWELVE HOURS OF GREEN HOUSES AND THE SIX SIGNS OF SAKE HOUSES, but a series that has however a great fame in Japan.

This painted monograph depicts, in twelve plates, the student of the silkworm.

The care of the breeder, says JAPAN AT THE WORLD FAIR, must be mainly in the selection of seeds and he must prefer cardboard from Yonesawa, Yamagawa, Neda; and seeds, (the first quality, can be recognized by the uniformity of the egg size, a purplish black color, and their adherence to the cardboard, whose touch does not detach them.

To hatch the eggs, the boxes are taken out of the boxes around March 20, and the seeds, which come in a bluish color, hatch on March 30, and the first board represents the workers, gently dropping the worms on a sheet of paper, which is covered with millet bran.

Plates 2 and 3 represent the harvesting of the mulberry tree and the chopping of the leaves, which are fed to the worms five times a day.

Then the first sleep, which takes place ten days after the hatching, and at the moment when the worm begins to take a whitish color: sleep during which a layer of rice bran is spread on the sheet of paper containing the worms, above which a net is stretched on which the worms rise, when they awaken. A second, third, fourth sleep follows in the boards, where, after three days, the worms are given whole mulberry leaves.

Then when the workers see the worms ready to spin, that they see them going up along the edges of the basket, they take them by hand, to put them in the *mabushi,* wavy straw, giving them all the possible facilities to spin.

And the last boards show us the enclosing of the silkworm in the cocoon, the transformation of the pupa into a butterfly, the sowing of eggs that a woman directs on paper, by a thread attached to the butterfly's leg, finally, the heating of the cocoons in boiling water, and the various manipulations, after which they become a band of cloth.

X

The history of painting in Japan, since it was painted there, from the end of the fifth century to the eighteenth, is in the succession of three schools.

In the beginning, it was the *Buddhist School*, a school that came out of the high plateaus of Asia, of learned India, and which, with the religion of Çakya Mouni, brought his painting to China, Japan and the whole Far East: painting representing the human being in a kind of sacred immobility, avoiding giving him the resemblance, refusing to make a portrait of him, depicting his face according to an art ritual, with systematic abbreviations, - and of the reality of his person, reproducing only the detail and richness of his clothes.

From this religious painting come out two profane schools.

The Tosa School, created by a member of the illustrious Foujivara family, at the end of the great civil wars, with fierce military fevers, in the middle of a society constituted, like our feudal Europe with its life as a castle. A school that makes lordly life, as well as battle life and the life of love and artistic retreat in the *yashiki,* precious in a style of aristocratic art, and of which the illustration of the love novel *Gen-zi Mono-gatari,* written by the poet Mura-saki Siki-bu, is a specimen that reveals the highest interest.

*The Kano School*16 created by Kano Massanobou, the national

---

[16] JAPANESE ART, by Louis Gonse. Quantin, 1883.

school in the eyes of the Japanese, the school of audacity and bravery of *doing*, the school sometimes with the crushing of the brush, sometimes with the tenuousness of a hair, the school with the initials of the line, the execution that we call Japanese, *gouantaï*, rocky, that is, hit, rough, with angular outlines: a school where there is a bit of an abuse of the process, of Japanese workshop *chic*, and still belonging entirely to an aristocratic aesthetic.

Basically, these two painters were, in their paintings and drawings, only painters of the noble classes, touching the other classes only with a finishing of their brush. However, it happened that in the last years of the seventeenth century, a defector of the Tosa school, Moronobou[17], breaking with the classical formulas, was the precursor of the school that Outamaro was really going to found.

And the school founded by Outamaro was the school of an art emerging from the convention, going to the people, and bringing the representation of intimate scenes of *vulgar life, in the* reality of poses, attitudes, movements, finally, giving the spectacle, so to speak, photographic of the inner existence of the woman of the Empire of the Sunrise: THE SCHOOL OF LIFE, *Ouki-yo-yé:* - *ouki,* meaning the one who floats above, who floats above; -yo, world, life, contemporary time; - *yé,* painting.

XI

In the plates dedicated to women, there is a series, what am I saying, a series, at least a hundred impressions, and which is called the "Great

---

[17] The Origins of Painting in History, by M. Bing, in Issues 13 and 14 of Japan Artistic.

Heads" collection, where the woman's head is represented, almost of natural size, with a little of her bust. These impressions, whose heads are always represented with this hieraticism that makes all heads almost identical, but with these fine arched eyebrows, one of the most appreciated beauties of women in Japan, have for us only the interest of the piece of dress that covers the shoulders, the chest of these women, the interest of the fan or the screen that they hold at their fingertips.

But in this grandeur, the perfection of the impression is admirable, and the embossing, this thing so unartistic in our country, so artistic in their country, putting the white relief of a chrysanthemum or cherry petal on a blue or purple dress, the white relief of an interlacing in a border, plays the trompe-l'oeil of a sample of a dress from there with the jump of its embroidery.[18]

These impressions of the "Great Heads" executed in large part, according to Hayashi, around 1795, are curious not only for their beauty, but also for the precious information they give us about the imitations, plagiarism, the theft of the artist's signature, made by his colleagues, and where Outamaro, to warn the public against the fakes circulating under his name, signs his Great Heads: *the true Outamaro.*

XII

According to the biographers, Outamaro's life is quite uniform: during the day he spends it at his publisher Tzutaya Jûzabro, where he

---

[18] The Japanese tried embossing, this introduction of relief into painting, even with great delicacy in the human figure, by detaching it from the outer contour of an ear, the aquiline curvature of a nose, the two flower petals with which they make the lips.

has a workshop; at night, he spends it at Yoshiwara. And the path is not long from the workshop to the Green Houses, because the house of its publisher is against the gate of the Yoshiwara. This explains the artist's in-depth knowledge of the *Quartier des Fleurs*.

XII

In this painter of the woman of the Green Houses, there is a curious side, it is the tendency of his brush to represent motherhood, to represent the mother in the tender occupation of her child.

There is nothing comparable in the images of Europe, to Outamaro's plates on breastfeeding. They are the head bending of our Virgin on the divine *bambino*; they are the ecstatic contemplation of the mother-feeder; they are the loving wraps of her arms, the delicate winding of one hand around an ankle, at the same time as the caress of the other behind the child's neck, suspended at her breast.

Outamaro paints us the mother cradling the child; the bathtub bathing him in the wooden tub, the country's bathtub; rolling him up, combing him between his teeth, his little tail; supporting him with a hand passed through his loose belt, his first steps; the fun of a thousand little games; making him take a marble in his mouth, giving him fear with, placed on his face, a mask of a fox, this legendary animal in the tales of the country's nurse, and even in the chapter of quadrupeds of THE JAPANESE ENCYCLOPEDIA, affirming that the fox blowing on the bones of a horse that he gnaws, makes a will-o'-the-wisp that illuminates him and that he lives a hundred years, and that he then greets the Great UR, and metamorphoses.

Between all these boards, a wonderful piece of reality is the one where a Japanese mother makes her child *pee, the* mother's two hands supporting the calves of the two legs spread apart from the child, while in a usual gesture in childhood, the two hands of the toddler play distractingly above her eyes.

In these assemblies, in these groups of mother and child, where the existence of the two beings is, so to speak, not yet completely separated, and where, from the mother's womb, the child's life seems to have passed on her knees, on her shoulders, one of the happiest boards is this one: a mother has her child on her back, leaning forward over her shoulder, and both look at each other in the water from the hollow of a tree trunk, and their two Ligurians seem to gather, move closer, almost kiss each other, in the reflection of this mirror of nature.

Among these expressions dedicated to motherhood, there is a series where the painter shows us, leaping above their mothers' heads, large children, with clogged arms and legs, with fat folds on their hocks and wrists, and who appear in their plethora of nudity, dressed only in a small apron, as one would dream of the children of their fat wrestlers.

There are still several other series devoted to the portrayal, of childhood in the woods, of a mahogany-skinned Herculean kid, which we see in *Yehon Sosi,* taking a young bear by the tail, and attracting it with violence to itself - a future hero - breastfed, fed, raised by a woman with a black hair, savagely disheveled, and whom we would mistake for a Genevieve of Brabant, from the time of the Cavern.

Here is, moreover, the story, quite legendary, of this kid, named Kintoki. Minamoto-no-Yorimitsu (died 1021) was once hunting on Ashighara Mountain in Saghami Province; finding no rare game there, he grew in the remotest parts of the mountain, and there he found a child with the muscles of a young Hercules, with a red skin, who played with a bear. When questioned by Yorimitsu, the child went to get his mother - the woman dressed in foliage and her terrible black hair, who, in noble language, in the language of the court, said that she did not want to make herself known. She is also known as *(Yama-ouwa (*mountain mother). However, the mountain mother agreed to Yorimitsu's request to take care of the child, telling him that he was the son of a great general of Minamoto, killed in a war against Taira, and that she raised him in the mountains, to make him a hero.

And the child who had grown up, soon took the name of Sakata-no-Kintoki, from the territory granted to him for his merits by Yorimitsu, who had made him one of his four great officers.

It was then that in the mountain of Oyéyama, in the province of Tampa, lived a great devil named Shûten-dôji, looting the surrounding provinces, shamelessly kidnapping young women there, and who, with his devils, beat the soldiers of the provincial governors. Complaints came to court, and Yorimitsu was charged with leading an expedition against the robber. But instead of taking an army corps with him, he was only accompanied by Kintoki and his three great officers, disguised as pilgrims. And having exhilarated the robbers with sake, and starting to dance with them, while Kintoki fought with Shutten-dôji with his wrist, and held him laughing in his hands, Yorimitsu suddenly pulled his sword like lightning, cut off his head so quickly, that, with his head cut off, they were still dancing at the end of the room, without suspecting the thing.

There followed a general battle, but the five heroes, among whom Kintoki worked wonders of value, took control of the devils demoralized by the death of their leader, and burned their lair, and brought the abducted women home.

Kintoki is still the hero of another adventure. Yorimitsu fell ill from an injury caused by a monster spider. And Kintoki and his three comrades managed to discover the nest of this gigantic spider, *tsusighumo,* and had the pleasure of killing her.

And here we are talking about Momotaro, the other legendary child who, with Kintoki, are the sweet children in honor of the Japanese children, and whose actions and gestures fill the albums intended for the children of this country.

The fable tells that there was once an old man and an old woman, and while the old man was cutting logs in the mountains, the old woman was washing clothes in the river. Now, while she was washing, she saw from afar, a big, huge red thing coming on the water, which she recognized as a catch, *momo,* but a very extraordinary catch. She was waiting for her husband to open it. And great was the astonishment of the old household to find a beautiful child there whom they named *Momotaro* (child of fishing). The child soon became a charming big boy. It was the time when the islanders of an island in the sea came to eat the inhabitants of the coast. He left for the island, with his dog, monkey and pheasant, and did such charming things with the help of the three animals, that the king of the island undertook not to come and eat the inhabitants anymore, and it is since that promise that Japan is without worry.

XIV

In the early years of this century, Outamaro's talent, in its incessant production, lost its originality. The artist ages with man.

He, so hostile to the representation of theatrical things, driven by the success of Toyokouni, who began to become his rival, he began to deal with subjects chosen from the plays, he performed *Miti-Yuki* (companions in love).

And in these and other compositions, the long women, the creatures slender in his first way, fatten, shear, thicken, and the feminine contours become fat in him, without having the fat of Kiyonaga.

Then, now, in his compositions, he introduces to his women, who alone filled the first imaginations of his brush, he introduces caricatured men, comic men, grotesque men[19], with the effect of contrasts, repellers.

The artist no longer has the attention to seduce by this ideal kindness, of which he clothed the woman, he strives, by the presence of these "bad men", to flatter the public of the time, more in love, in the image, with comedy than real beauty, - the public of the time, whose taste is compared by Hayashi, to the taste of some modern ivory collectors in Yokohama who, he says, "prefer the grimace to art".

XV

But now, at this moment of the exhaustion of Outamaro's verve, a book is published, where he brings to the public a documentary illustration of the dwelling of his nights and days, and which makes the famous painter, a quite popular painter.

This book is the *Sei-rôyé-hon Nen-jû Ghiô-jï*

Sei - green

Jiô - two-storey house

Yé - drawing

---

[19] There is in Outamaro, during the golden age of his talent, such resistance to put in the midst of his women, a man, a naughty man, that in the triptych board of his Grand Bridge over the Soumida, the man who holds a parasol over a woman's head, is so cleverly hidden, that if we do not pay great attention to looking at the image, we can believe that this parasol stands alone on his head.

Hon - book

Nen - year

Day - in

Ghio - what's going on

Jï - thing

Book whose current translation is:

DIRECTORY OF GREEN HOUSES, but whose verbatim translation would be more like: *Illustrated book of* things that happen during the year in Green Houses.

Now from this book, printed in color, and composed of two volumes of our small in-octavo format, let us give a detailed description according to the indications provided by the publisher.

The text is by Jipensha Ikkou.

The drawings are by Kitaghawa Mourasaki-ya Outamaro with the collaboration of her students:

Kikumaro.

Hidémaro.

Takimaro.

The wood engraver is called Foujï Katzumouné.

The shooter of the Kwak-shôdô Tôyémon boards.

Publisher Kasoûsaya Tusouké (artist name Jou-ô), living in Yédo, main street of the Japanese Bridge (Nihonbashi).

The book was printed for the new year 1804.

The book's cover, made of soft blue paper, is embossed with lanterns worn on the Yoshiwara promenades, bearing the coats of arms of celebrities of the Green Houses of the Year[20]. The back cover of the first volume carries the command screen, which is held in his hand by the wrestler judge. In this screen, printed in red, is in the middle the title of the book, flanked to the right and left by the names of Outamaro and Jipensha Ikkou, as a tribute to their talent, at the same time as the representation of this screen means that the book is carried as the judge of the Yoshiwara.

The poetry square, at the top of the first volume, is decorated with a flowering apple branch and a red camellia stem. The verses are from Sandara-hôshi, who says:

"O, *dawn bell, if you understood the heavy heart of farewells*, you *would gladly read a lie, instead of ringing the six bells.* »

The poetry square at the top of the second volume, surrounded by chrysanthemums and *momichi,* contains a description of the Soumida River at the Yoshiwara.

The frame of the table of contents represents the gate of the Yoshiwara enclosure. The top lines for text, the bottom lines for illustrations.

At the end of the second volume, a second edition of a second series of the book is announced, a publication that did not appear because of a discussion between the writer and the artist. Jipenska Ikkou, attributing the success of the book to his prose, Outamaro to his illustration.

From the DIRECTORY OF GREEN HOUSES, printed in color, there are a few copies in black, one of which I own: a copy from which Outamaro and his colleagues first had a small number drawn, for their

---

[20] In Japan, the coat of arms is not the exclusive attribute of the nobility; all classes have a right to it, and even the Yeta, the Japanese pariahs, relegated far from their compatriots' homes, carry coats of arms.

use, to try to use watercolor to color the printed plates.

In the preface, the preface by Senshûro tells us that, although this book is called a directory, it is not the same as the court of the Emperors of the fourteenth century, where the text is composed only of small poems, but that on the contrary this new directory is inspired by real life, *a real joyful crowd life.* And he adds that the book gives the animated physiognomy of Yoshiwara, during the four seasons by the *elegant brush of* Outamaro, for illustration, and by the spiritual pen-brush of Jipensha Ikkou, for the text.

First some explanations. Europe has very misconceptions about Japanese prostitution, at least about prostitution dating back to the last century and the early years of this century. The fifty Green Houses of the Yoshiwara, and the hundreds outside the enclosure, owed their sumptuous existence and splendor above all to the rich population of Yedo, not to foreigners, but to the ambassadors, provincial and commercial businessmen, of the three hundred and sixty accredited princes, near the Shogun, who lived in its capital without their families. Then the woman of the Green House is not the low prostitute like the prostitute of our country, the woman we own when we cross the threshold of the house, the woman "out of class, the woman of the *nagaya*", as we call her and that she exists there. The woman of the Green House is the courtesan.

And the origin and the consecration of these courtesans in the house, is lost in the mists of time. We can see their existence under Emperor Shômou, from the eighth century, and *Man-yô- shû, a* collection of ancient poems, is full of pieces that celebrate them.

It was under Shôji-Jin-yemon, that the Yoshiwara of Yédo was created, around 1600, by order of the administrative authority. The site was then very close to the Shogun's residence. Later, in 1657, following a major fire, new land was granted in the suburb of Assa Kousa, where a neighborhood was built enclosed within a compound, and in the eighth month of this year the inauguration of the Yoshiwara took place. The houses are separated by five streets, the main street of which is the rue du Milieu, where there are only tea houses[21] *(tchaya)*, on the front throughout the street. And the cleanliness and beauty of these tea houses, which occupy both sides of Middle Street, raise doubts, according to the expression of Jipensha Ikkou, as to *whether one is on earth. The* regulation of the Yoshiwara is found in the *Daïsen,* and the *Saïken* contains, in the most detailed way, all the names of the courtesans and musicians of the tea houses.

Moreover, about these women who are so much involved in Japanese painting and poetry, listen to the author of the text of the Green Houses:

The daughters of the Yoshiwara are raised as princesses. From childhood onwards, they are given the most complete education. We teach them reading, writing, arts, music, tea, perfume (the game of perfumes is like the game of the drawee: we compose the perfumes we burn, and we have to guess at the smell of these perfumes). *They are quite like princesses, raised at the bottom of palaces... Then why look at an expense of a thousand rios?* A rio of Koban is worth one-pound sterling.

And here is a very particular detail. These women, who came from the different provinces of the "Sunrise" Empire with their patois, have unlearned it, this patois, and speak an archaic language special to Yoshiwara: the noble language, the poetic language, the language of the court from the seventh to the ninth century, a little modernized.

However, between these daimios, these literate lords and these women who had received an education from great courtesans, "the

---

[21] The tea house is only a restaurant, a café.

contact of the two epidermis" did not take place immediately, because these prostitutes in houses had in the choice, a little freedom of free prostitution in our country. Indeed, the plates of this suite of Outamaro show you the formalities of relationships, the kind of ceremonial that presides over them, and the three almost indispensable visits, to reach intimacy: the first visit, which is only a gallant introduction to the woman, the second, which is the *doubling of the* first visit, with the granting of some privacies, and finally the third visit, called the visit of ripe knowledge.

Now it would perhaps not be without interest to give a plan of these houses of pleasure, the largest houses of Yédo, of these houses containing ten to twenty first-class courtesans, containing fifty to sixty second class courtesans, each having a small apartment.

They are almost all houses retreating on the sidewalk, and this small setback is planted with shrubs putting greenery and Hours on the front of the house.

The entrance is usually on the right. It is behind a sliding door, made of artistically crafted trellis, an antechamber with a clay floor, at the bottom of which there is a stone step, on which one places one's shoes, the *quêta* and *zori,* the *quêta* in fine straw, the *zori in* wood. From there, we enter the large living room, a kind of *hall,* on the floor like all the other rooms, covered with *tatami,* thin white mats, lined with a very tight rice straw, seven centimeters thick, on which the walk is all soft.

In the middle stands the staircase leading up to the upper floors, to the bedrooms: this staircase is still represented in the images of the Green Houses, with courtesans leaning over the ramp at the top, for their tender farewells to the customers.

The large lounge communicates with two or three small lounges, which are places where customers are kept waiting when there are too many people in the large lounge.

On the left is the office with the cash register, and on the right and back on the garden, the room where the employees stand, the dining room, the bathrooms, the kitchen.

Except for a few rooms, given to the privileged ones of the house, who want to be on the same level as the garden, all the women's apartments are on the first and second floors.

Behind the house extend beyond the open-air galleries, these large gardens, represented in the prints, flowered in pink, framing the light architecture, filled with light and sunlight entering through the huge bays, through the window walls.

Here are the ten impressions that form the illustration of the first volume:

I.   New Year's Day wishes in Nakano-chô (Middle Street).

II.   Inauguration of the new covers.

III.   Beginning of a *schinzo*.

IV.   And V. Women's exposure at night to the bays overlooking the street.

V.   The blossoming of the rue du Milieu.

VI.   The absence of the mistress of the Green House.

VII. Beginning of a singing musician.

VIII.   Lantern Festival.

IX.   Niwaka. (The impromptu party or Carnival.)

FIRST IMPRESSION
New Year's Wishes.

On the first day of New Year's Eve, it is a great entertainment in Yoshiwara.

For five days, we have been *decorating the pine tree,* planting in front of the houses, large branches in the middle of bamboo sections, connected by ropes.

A plantation, where in the setting of the Green Houses, the Japanese take the greatest care to ensure that the pine branches face the entrance to the houses and turn their backs on the street, following the superstitious idea that "turning their backs" is, all over the world, the negation of love.

It is the second day that the courtesans leave, to wish in the streets of the Middle, the New Year to their acquaintances of the other houses. An exit called *Dô-tchù* (travel), which comes and goes between the cross streets of Kioto and Yédo.

A toilet competition, where each establishment has its own particular style, where each woman is left free to her own taste, and where old habits are preserved, and where the Shôyôro house has kept the sandals of yesteryear, and has not replaced them with lacquered wooden shoes *(kamagheta)*, invented by Fouyô de Hishiga, is worn today by everyone.

And it is all this day, in the rue du Milieu, a procession, *where the silk sleeves shine, and where the embroidered dresses spread in the air the most delicious perfumes.*

SECOND PRINTING
Inauguration of the new coverage[22].

---

[22] The European bed is unknown in Japan. This cotton wool mattresses, called fton, stored in cupboards during the day, are spread out in the evening on mats on *tatami*. Their thickness is 2 to 3 centimeters. Rarely do we use more than one or two. There are no sheets. The envelope of the futon is made of cotton or silk; in winter, it is fully dressed, more or less naked, in summer. The

The new blankets and cushions, offered by the friend of heart, are displayed in the main living room of the house. And there, the courtesan is congratulated on the beautiful things she has received, and it is the occasion of a small celebration, for which the mistress of the house sends her most excellent fish, her best sake.

While the courtesan receives these objects at night in her apartment, she makes gifts to the women and men employed in the house. And the first night she tries on her blanket and pillow, it is customary for her to be polite enough to send the buckwheat or rice cake to everyone in the house and to friends.

For his part, the friend of heart has the duty to distribute dyed cotton scarves, where the coats of arms of the lover and the courtesan are intertwined. And on the other hand, the employees of the house offer him, as well as a *wedding display,* a box where a branch of pine, bamboo, plum tree are planted, and to thank them, the lover distributes them the *bouquet* (flower in Japanese), because the silver gift was called flower in this refined world. Moreover, at that time, in these places of pleasure, there was a certain modesty about the question of money. During the hours or days spent with the courtesan, money was never taken out of her pocket, and never asked for by women, only paid the

---

cover is represented by another futon that has the shape of a houppelande and has sleeves. The pillow, called a makoura, is a wooden block, 10 to 12 centimeters high, with a 20 centimeters long upper surface and 5 centimeters wide, carrying a small cylindrical cushion, wrapped in paper, and held by the middle. The makoura, a real torture for a European... It was once necessary for Japanese of both sexes, because of the complicated hairstyles, which were only renewed every two or three days.

house bill at the exit.

Basically, this day of the new cover was very favorable to the woman's reputation, when the bedding was rich, distinguished, sumptuous. *And it is on that day, says the author of the* Green Houses, *that the unused man who asks for a second baguette to eat, when offered baguettes that open in two, who asks to be served something better, when served an* arami (fish with tender bones), ... *that the repulsive man, whom the unpleasant man can win by his gift, the heart of the courtesan...*

And Jipensha Ikkou adds: In *this world, it is essentially necessary to take care of the external radiance of your friend. Be generous with the expense, and don't neglect any attention. In great circumstances, stay ahead of your rivals, and be loved by employees; by offering them* the bouquet *from time to time. As long as you are well seen and well known in the house, you can do anything, and then everything is fun for you.*

THIRD PRINTING

Beginning of a Shinzô.

The great courtesan is called *Oïran.* Each Oïran has under his direction two girls, named *Kamourô.* The Kamourôs arrived at a certain age and became Schinzôs. Later, they started and became Oïrans. There, the formalities of this ceremony are given, where it is a question of the blackening of the teeth, this distinctive sign of married women. When a Japanese person is in contact with a schinzô, a past Oïran, and is willing to pay for the operation, he can get her to have her teeth blackened. So, it is a kind of marriage valid in Yoshiwara, and the courtesan cannot accept a serious friend offer, or at least with the knowledge of the man who paid for the blackening of his teeth. Yeah, she's supposed to have no other relationships.

FOURTH AND FIFTH IMPRESSIONS

Women's exposure at night
to the latticed windows of the house overlooking the street.

The descriptor, after a praise of Outamaro and a brief description of these two plates, which are small masterpieces, seeks to guide the choice of the passer-by among these women, through rather psychological observations.

The one who immerses herself in reading a book, without worrying about the chatter of others, is the one who will most pleasantly entertain you once you have entered her intimacy.

The one who, from time to time, whispers with her neighbors, hides her face to stifle her laughter, and looks at a man in the white of her eyes, is able to roll you with a surprising trick ...

The one who has her hands in her dress, at chest height, and her chin in her neck, and looks long into the air, is the one who suffocates her heartache. *Oh, she won't be funny the first few times, but the day you win her heart, she won't let you go.* The *one who chats, jokes and laughs with the submistress, and suddenly turns around, to hear a passer-by's chorus, is a very capricious creature. If you are to his liking, you will be his darling right away... The one who writes several letters is the woman who wants to make a clientele. Becoming her lover of heart, will be difficult, but if you are old, ugly, unable to be loved by other women, you will have with her the all-powerful shine of your gold.... The one who, still young, spends her time playing, has remained an innocent, you can do with her what you want....*

SIXTH PRINTING

The planting of cherry trees in Nakano-chô.

During the third month (front page calendar), cherry blossoms are laid all along rue du Milieu, and it is a busy day, full of walkers.

A large composition of Toyokouni, a band of five boards, represents this plantation and the walk that takes place there. This plantation is curious, because at the moment when their flower shoots begin, the cherry trees are planted in the ground, and there is a park alley that is nothing like a city street, and in this kind of improvised forest, it is a coming and going of superb courtesans, in the small procession of their kamourôs and shinzôs, hardly making a passage, through the crowd of Japanese, young and old, throwing them in the passage of looks and loving compliments. And it is really charming the spectacle of the seabed, where through the snow bloom of the cherry trees, covering everything, there are the appearance of laughing corners of houses, bits of roofs, pretty pieces of women.

SEVENTH IMPRESSION

The absence of the mistress of the house.

A board that Jipensha-Ikkou does not describe is a board, where the housewife's exit, probably for an excursion in the countryside, during the flowering season of cherry trees or chrysanthemums, leads to a wonderful hide and seek, in which women who flee the hand that will grab them, fall flat on their stomachs.

EIGHTH IMPRESSION

Beginning of a musician singer.

It was in the large living room, in the middle of the general curiosity of the women, and with their heads stretched through the in-between doors, that the singer began, preceded by a distribution of screens where her name was written, in the middle of verses celebrating her person and her talent.

NINTH IMPRESSION

The lantern festival.

This feast, called Torô, which takes place in the middle of summer, shows the whole house, busy tying lanterns. And in this festival the lanterns have painted, on their enlightened transparency, the most amusing caricatures.

TENTH IMPRESSION

Niwaha (the improvised party or carnival).

A carnival from there, where all the singers are dressed as men, with their hair cut like young boys.

Now here is the illustration of the second volume which contains only nine plates.

I.   The first day of the eighth month.

II.   Contemplation of the full moon.

III.   The first interview.

FIRST IMPRESSION

The first day of the eighth month.

In the great heat of the month (end of August and beginning of September), it is the ceremony of the white costume, the wearing by all the women of white dresses, that they will walk, one day, in the street of the Middle: an exhibition of dresses-paintings, which has around it the curiosity of the whole city. For this walk of a few hours, white dresses were painted by the greatest Japanese painters, and in a special book on courtesans, there is a dress engraved after Korin, which the painter had decorated for the famous Ousougboumô.

SECOND PRINTING

Contemplation of the moon.

An impression, where you can see courtesans on a terrace with lovers, eyes in the sky, contemplating a beautiful summer night.

Yes, - this is noted by Jipensha-Ikkou, - their education has endowed the women of the Yoshiwara with a poetic feeling, and the silvery light of the night star, in the melancholic serenity of the beautiful summer nights, makes them spread, these improvised poets of the Moon, in the dreams of an elegiac lyricism.

And these are the verses of the courtesan Kumai: "It is *only by* admiring the Moon together that it is beautiful to me. When I'm alone, she inspires too many tender feelings in me! »

And the verses of the courtesan Azuma:

"*And tonight, to whom will be the sweetness of my being, in this passing world, with my floating body.* »

And the verses of the courtesan Kameghiku:

Oh! that the reflection of the moonlight is brilliantly reflected on the water of the Soumida (just like its existence), *but that autumn on the other side of the clouds* (honest life) *makes me envy it!* »

And the verses of the courtesan Miyako:

"*Although I am only a woman of nothing, down here on earth, the Moon illuminates my heart with a comforting ray.*

And the verses of the courtesan Miyaghino:

"*How many times do I separate myself from man, whose shadow I can no longer see, under the moon of the dawn[23]?* »

THIRD PRINTING

The first interview,
the first acquaintance, the first night.

On the first night, if the person who is laughing does not like it, the courtesan is free not to spend it with him.

And this is an opportunity to recall this story, which would not be a legend. The famous Takao, quoted in the *Kwaghai Maurokou,* refused Prince Dati of Sendaï, because of her passion for a lover of hearts. The prince having used all means in vain to get her, invited her to a boat

---

[23] THE FIFTY COURTESAN POETESSES. - NOTES ON THE QUARTIER DES FLEURS.

trip, and after killing her, threw her into the Soumida.

"If you are not approved the first time, and you are patient," says Jipensha-Ikkou,"you can, in the second visit, complete the *repetition* formality. *At the* third visit, it is necessary to reach *mature knowledge. It is of* course understood that for those who were able to sleep the first time, the *doubling of the* visit is required.

A rather curious and unknown detail is that the Japanese making a station in a Green House, changes costume, takes, it is the expression, the uniform of the house: this costume making there, each man is equal to any other man.

FOURTH PRINTING
Knowledge matures.

Mature knowledge" preceded by a face-to-face dinner, where people eat from bowls and plates bearing the woman's coat of arms, and where ivory sticks are used, the use of which is considered a marriage commitment. It is followed, this mature knowledge, by a *general bouquet,* i.e. a distribution of money to all the employees, men and women of the house, who are sometimes fifty in the big houses. And after that evening and night, he said to himself: *Madam has made a serious friend.*

And if the one who has come to mature knowledge can pay the costs of two or three days' or a week's stay, it is, according to the expression in the printout, the *enjoyment of a married life, which is nothing more than a series of hobbies and distractions in pleasure.*

FIFTH IMPRESSION

The next morning.

The fifth board represents the morning of the night spent in the Green House. Cleaning the house, preparing a cup of tea, while, despite the inner happiness of the book, *the serious friend,* sitting on the edge of a paper window, looks melancholy at the snowy landscape, brushing his teeth.

SIXTH PRINTING
The renewal.

The putting on the shoulders of the latter's dress, the hooding of the latter by another woman, the tender "goodbye" to a last one by a third woman, graciously supported with both hands on the staircase, finally all the pretty amiabilities of the farewell.

SEVENTH IMPRESSION

The Kouronwa penalty (Yoshiwara Precinct.)

When a Japanese man has given his coat of arms (family or invention) to a courtesan, and has made her unfaithful, it is a great shame for the woman. So, she has the right to punish him! To this end, she distributes within the compound the wives of her friends who are watching for the infidel, discover the house where he is going, wait for his exit, seize his person by force, take him to the courtesan, where he is made all the miseries imaginable, not too mean, however.

And the seventh board gives you the representation of the guilty person, dressed as a girl, dressed as Kamourô, asking, kneeling, for forgiveness, in the laughter of all the women shared by the oïran, victim of his treason.

EIGHTH IMPRESSION

The manufacture of rice cakes at the end of the year.

The eighth board introduces you to the middle of making rice cakes for New Year's Day, with everyone in the household: women, servants, maidservants, children, working on making large and small cakes.

NINTH IMPRESSION

The painting of a Ho-ô (fabulous bird) in a Green House.

In the childish admiration of women, one of whom, to see more closely, is on all fours on the floor, a painter is painting on a whole panel of a wall of the courtesans' exhibition room, a gigantic Ho-O - a painter who, by his habits, could very likely be Outamaro[24].

At the time the book of Green Houses was published, women involved in prostitution in Yoshiwara were divided into four classes.

The first: the women of *Nakano-chô* (those who go for the big walk);

The 2nd: the women of *Tchônami* (a class enjoying more or less the same consideration as the first);

The 3rd: the women of *Koghôshi* (the small grid);

---

[24] This last plate of the second volume of Outamaro is not mentioned in the illustration room. Moreover, this table is rather carelessly made, and the text and illustrations do not always match.

The 4th: the women of *Kiri-Missé* (retail store).

The number of first-class houses was one-third of the second, the number of second-class houses was only one-tenth of the third, and the number of fourth-class houses was one-quarter higher than the third.

So, there were very few first-class houses, and the number of great courtesans was very limited, and in general, it was only the great courtesans that the painters' brush, like Outamaro, reproduced.

Basically, out of a population of two million inhabitants, which numbered Yedo at the end of the eighteenth century and in the first years of the nineteenth century, there were only 6,300 women in Yoshiwara, and of these 6,300 women, there were only 2,500 prostitutes of all classes[25].

Now, at the service of the Green Houses, there are two classes of men and women, whose responsibilities are rather poorly defined, and

---

[25] As we can see, prostitution did not have, does not even have today such a great development as claimed by travelers of the past century, of the present century. This is an opportunity for Mr. Hayashi to rise in a note, following the translation of the book of Jipenscha Ikkou, against the accusation of immorality made in Japan, and to shout that the English who spent a week in Paris, declare that it is the most corrupt city on the continent, and to wonder, what a Frenchman of the English would think if he were transported to London, in certain streets, at nine in the evening. And he affirms that Buddhism and *Confucianism* have brought to his nation such elements of morality that if there were a way, according to his expression, to *wash the hearts,* Japan's *moral detergent* would be the least dirty of the detergents made in the five parts of the world.

And in the revolt of his patriotism, he mistreats, in a very amusing little tone of anger, our friend Loti, accusing him of having mistaken for a great courtesan, a *"reshamen"* (literally sheep), a gallant woman of an inferior race, and for the special use of foreigners.

whose living conditions are very little known in Europe: the *taikomati* and the *guesha.*

The *taikomati* was a kind of funny companion, a funny mahout, an elegant cicerone of prostitution, prayed as well as the *guesha,* at the wedding salon, by invitation of the tea house, and charged with bringing joy to the meeting. These *taikomati* were, say the Japanese, very intelligent, very spiritual men, aware of everything that was happening in Yedo. And men of a character who can never get angry with them. Then a discretion to which everything could be entrusted, and any secret, without the slightest fear! People with a word that could easily be relied on, and therefore honesty, turned into a proverb! They accepted nothing but the pledge paid by the house, and the *flower* (the silver roll) that it is customary to offer them.

The *taikomati,* in their low profession, had a very good education, a very sufficient education, an education maliciously compared to the education of a candidate who failed at the Seïdô academy (the scientific center of Yédo). And even outside of Yoshiwara, for whom it was a little silvery, there was an interest in hiring a taikomati for a boat trip, for an excursion on the Soumida dam, because there was not a minute of trouble with this devil of a man, who was just talkative only as much as you wanted, and who had the talent to make himself, with great tact, the companion with your mood. A real resource that this man, when you had drunk too much, to correct the mistakes of the note, and put your wallet and valuables in his pocket, safely! Relax on the seawall, in a tea house, to better admire the Soumida through the snowy pink landscape of cherry blossoms? you were the first to be served, in the middle of the crowd. Did you enter a restaurant? You had the best cabin, and the menu ordered by your companion was executed perfectly. Moreover, they were known everywhere, and a house badly seen by the taikomati could not work. Were you in a large guesha society, there was a need for a taikomati to take over the management, and everything was going well, and he put the whole guesha troop in a good mood. A science apart, a science by him acquired in Yoshiwara that made the pleasures with the price of his services cost you less expensive, than if you took care of the expense by yourself.

The *taikomati* knew how to sing, dance and act, but they were careful, in their talent for pleasure, never to shade the *guesha*, and they never condescended to take up service in second-class green houses. The people accompanying people attending this class are called *Nodaiko,* who has the despicable sense of *taiko of* the fields, *taiko* not belonging to the Yoshiwara.

The *guesha*[26]*,* singers or dancers who frequent the main street in the middle, are called *kemban.* They always go, two by two, having the prohibition to sleep with a man from the city in Yoshiwara, and this surveillance of one by the other, saves them from occasions when they could weaken[27]. In the case of weakness, the singer is expelled from the Yoshiwara. In general, their conduct is considered irreproachable, and this is the explanation for so many marriages of women of this class with very distinguished men.

The *guesha* and *taikomati* are under the direction of the artists' central office, located in Nakanochô. In this office, the wooden cards in which the names are written hang in alphabetical order. The invitation to the tea house arrives, formulated in a letter containing the names of the requested singers. And as soon as the commitment is made, the cards

---

[26] Mr. Hayashi observed that there are still all the types of *guesha that* Outamaro reproduced at the beginning of the century.

[27] It is said that these women take a vow of chastity until the time of their marriage, which can only take place when they leave a tea house.

of the names involved are removed and placed under the cards of the Green Houses, which are located on another wall: a very ingenious bookkeeping.

Second class houses have singers attached to the house, and who live there.

Green Houses cannot directly invite *guesha or taikomati: it is* always through the artists' office that the invitation is made. We cannot extend beyond known hours, except in the case of a major fire[28], and if this happens, the *thayra* must pay compensation, and it is refused the engagement of artists, for a period of time indicated by the regulations.

When you come to invite the *guesha* for a game outside the Yoshiwara, you have to order several days in advance, and through the house, and the *guesha go for a* walk or a short trip with you, always accompanied by an employee of the tea house and one or two box holders of the three-string musical instrument, called schamisen.

A curious recommendation. The *taikomati* and *guesha*, who are in the courtesans' apartments, owe them the respect that a servant owes to the master, for it is customary for great courtesans to be treated like princesses.

XVI

The Yoshiwara was painted by all Japanese painters. Kitao Massanobou made the: NEW ILLUSTRATION OF THE

---

[28] Mr. Rodolphe Lindau writes that during a fairly long stay in Yédo, there was barely a night without him hearing the bell ringing, and affirms that the average age of Japanese houses does not exceed fifteen years.

BEAUTIFUL LITERATE WOMEN OF YOSHIWARA; Shunshô and Shighemasa : THE MIRROR OF GREEN HOUSES; Hokkei : THE TWELVE HOURS AT YOSHIWARA; Harunobou : THE BEAUTIFUL WOMEN OF GREEN HOUSES, etc., etc.. I stop..., know that Mr. Hayashi has, in the library he owns in Japan, more than two hundred books about the elegant prostitution district.

But for almost all Japanese painters, the images of the Yoshiwara are pretexts for groups of women who are a little ideal, for sumptuous *theories* in the middle street, for exhibitions of bright embroidered dresses, for the pictorial staging of women who do not mean the habits, the characters, the profession of the courtesan of the Yoshiwara.

There is hardly any painter, there is hardly any Outamaro, who tells with drawing and color, the private life of these women, day and night, - and makes us curious! -the rival painter of Outamaro, the painter whose long and slender figures of Japanese women sometimes leave you uncertain in the attribution, and make you look for the signature, yes, Toyokouni has published a book on Green Houses. And it is really interesting to study this book, and to compare it to the Outamaro book, especially since both books are from the same period; the Green Houses of Outamaro having been published in 1804 and the Green Houses of Toyokouni in 1802.

But before analyzing this book, I would like, to give an idea of this prostitution, so different from the brutally sensual prostitution of the West, to show a side of the almost poetic prostitution of the Empire of the Sunrise, of prostitution, with this prostitute's room where there are musical instruments and a library, although the document that I republish, after M. Rosny, more recent than the illustrations of Outamaro and Toyokouni, and a time when the infiltration of foreigners into Yoshiwara [29] is beginning to take place.

This document is a popular, Sino-Japanese folk song called: STUDY OF FLOWERS IN YOSHIWARA. Listen to this song: "Look at these two pretty butterflies on this flower. Why do they fly without separating?

——   It is, undoubtedly, because the weather is beautiful, and they have been intoxicated by the scent of the flowers.

——   We too, like these butterflies, are going to visit the flowers.

——   Have you studied the science of flowers?

——   I studied it under the guidance of an excellent master of Yoshiwara.

——   There's the big door.

——   Don't you know any teachers?

——   I know Professor Komourasaki (Dark Purple).

——   Please wait a moment, Professor Ousougoumo (Light Clouds), will come.

——   The professor is long overdue; I have no idea why?

——   Yoshiwara's teachers are wasting a lot of time because of the complications of their bathing. First, they like to use, for the arrangement of their hairstyle, Simomoura ointment and Tsyôzi cords. [30]

---

[29]   Here is the description as the crow flies of Yoshiwara by Mr. Rodolphe Lindau in 1865:

"Yoshiwara forms a kind of separate city, isolated from Yedo by walls and ditches; you enter through a single gate, which is guarded night and day by a police station. It is a regular parallelogram, measuring one quarter kilometer in circumference. Four longitudinal streets and three transverse streets, cut at right angles, divide it into nine districts separated by wooden grids, which are closed at will, and which allow for strict surveillance."

[30]   In Japanese: *moto-yui, it is a* kind of small cord with which the Japanese tie their hair.

Some are adopting Katsouyama's fashion, others prefer Simada's. They do not realize that their flake comb and coral head needles, for which they spend a thousand pounds, increase their debts. Rice powder for the face, rice powder for the neck, blush for the lips, and even black for the teeth[31], there is nothing in them that does not detect prodigality.

A moment later, the teacher introduced himself.

In truth, he is very pretty, distinguished, kind. To his eyebrows is drawn the mist of distant mountains, to his eyes the quivering waves of autumn; his profile is high, his mouth small, the whiteness of his teeth shame the snow of Fuzi-Yama; the charms of his body remind us of the willow tree, during the summer. Her outer garment is adorned with flying dragons, embroidered in gold thread on black velvet. She wears a golden brocade belt; in a word, her toilet is perfect.

—— I have come to speak with you to begin the study of flowers.

—— But have you thought this study through, how tiring is it?

Please come to my room.

The description of these rooms being known to everyone, it is useless to talk about them in detail. On the platform[32], which was arranged to accommodate six mats, three blinds by the painter Hôïtsou[33], representing flowers and birds, were hung. We put away the

---

[31] In Japanese; *ha-guro.* This is a kind of powder that Japanese women are used to using to blacken their teeth.

[32] In Japanese room dwellings, there is a raised part of the room, where the mats that serve as a bed are usually placed.

[33] Famous painter from Yédo.

sougorokou[34] game, the *go* game of utensils to warm up tea, a harp, a guitar, a violin. Next to it, in a library, we find from the famous history of the Ghenzi, Mourasaki Sibikou[35] to the novels of Taménaga Siomisoui[36].

This is the room, and this is the courtesan's bathroom, as well as the honest woman's, the elegant looking bathroom.

A small window, about seventy centimeters high and projecting from the outside, and closed with a very artistic bamboo mesh, forms the toilet table on its inside edge. A kind of copper cauldron is used as a basin for washing. A wooden bucket, surrounded by bamboos, contains the water that is transferred by means of a long-handled bucket.

The woman's toiletries are in a small piece of furniture made of black and gold lacquer. A metal mirror is placed on a lacquered easel and covered with a piece of embroidered silk. This small piece of furniture also contains the women's ornaments, which consist of combs made of turtle shell, gold lacquer in the most varied patterns, and hairpins made of gold, silver, - the only jewelry of Japanese women.

However, when the teacher presents himself for the second time, he is dressed in his bed clothes, including a red crepe cap, topped with a

---

[34] A kind of backgammon game for which dice are used.

[35] A kind of very complicated checkers game, which consists in winning ground, while taking as many prisoners as possible to the opponent. Two-color tokens are used

[36] In Japanese *Gen-zi-mono-galari*. It is the romantic story of the famous family of Ghenzi or Minamoto, which originated from the daughters of the Mikado Saga (810 to, 823). The author, Muqra-saki Siki-bu, who lived under the reign of itsi-doô (987-1011), was one of the most sought-after women in the court for both her beauty and her talent.

purple satin nightgown, adorned with peonies and lions[37] embroidered with gold threads. He lets his dark hair fall back, capable of chaining the hearts of a thousand men, and allows us to see a body whose whiteness would mortify the snow itself. His face, with the smile of a plum tree, is similar to pear blossoms, enameled with raindrops.

- The flower is weak; please water it often.

Speaking in this way, the peach blossom blushed, like the sun when it sets[38].

Let us return to the painter Toyokouni, to the illustration of his book entitled: TODAY'S MORES *(Yèhon Imayô-sugata)*, whose first volume represents honest women of all conditions, but whose second volume is entirely devoted to the Yoshiwara.

She is the great courtesan, when she goes out for a walk in the rue du Milieu, between her two shinzôs, one of whom is putting the finishing touches to her toilet and having her two little kamourôs following her who are about to follow her.

It is the *shea,* the submistress, an elderly woman, in charge beyond the direction of the house, telling the ear of the great courtesan, that she is asked in the living room.

It is the festival of the carnival, as it is more or less reproduced by Outamaro, in the middle of the contribution of large lacquered wooden crates, containing the *schamisen,* and with the *guesha,* as boys.

A brown lacquered board, where you can write with a brush loaded

---

[37] It is a mistake, the Japanese have never painted lions, the dress represents Fô dogs, in the middle of a field of peonies.

[38] JAPANESE ANTHOLOGY. Ancient and modern poems from the Nippon Islanders, translated into French by Léon de Rosny. Paris, Maison neuve et Cie. 1871.

with white, the things to do, the orders to give, the small daily events. Below, the money chest on which there is a roll of letter paper, a writing table, a rolled kakemono, a closed fan, a small tea pot (*tchiaré*) in his silk bag.

In a corner, above a cabinet, the arrangement of an altar, at the bottom of which stands a small pagoda, surrounded by torches for illumination, and in front of a bottle of sake in the middle of letters containing silver gifts (bouquets). On the wall, hung, rows of paper cocoas, rows of small red circles, representing embryonic little children, which are good luck charms, and with these good luck charms, another Okamé mask, whose smile in the vestibule of the houses is, as we have already said, in the belief of the Japanese, an invitation to the good mood of the visitor. "A *smile,*" said the first king of Japan, Ooanamouti, "*is the source of happiness and fortune.* »

In the middle of the room, the mistress sits with her hand resting on her pipe, straight on the ground, while a servant massages her shoulders, and a woman lying flat on her stomach examines silk squares, lying on the mat of the floor.

These four Toyokouni boards show us the prostitution of the first class, but with the fifth board, we enter the prostitution of the second, the third class,- and this fifth board, it is the women's showroom, from where through the bars of the closure, a fortune teller predicted from the street, to women, the future.

Then it is the interior of his house[39], during the unoccupied hours,

---

[39] Here is the rather sad picture that Mr. Rodolphe Lindau makes of one of these exhibitions, in his TRIP AROUND JAPAN, published in 1804: "We had approached one of these *djorodja,* and through the bars of the gate, we distinguished a spacious room, furnished with bamboo mats, and poorly lit by four large lanterns made of colored paper. Next to us were a dozen Japanese

where we see women in tired poses, kneeling on the edge of the big bay, looking stupidly at the landscape, or sitting on that edge, their backs turned to the street, stretching nervously, or leaning over terrines, greedily eating little boiled crabs, while in the background we see one, with her body wiggled, her neck twisted, her mouth wide open, her little ridiculous nose in the air, and her eyebrows in circumferential accents, in her musical delirium, slurping in the most drollish way, frenetically accompanied by the *schamisen*.

I mean, it's the life of those women in the gardens.

And it is a woman showing another the love tattoo of her arm, bearing the name of her lover of heart, sometimes her initial, her coat

---

people who, with their faces against the grid, examined, like us, what was happening in the room. There were eight young girls there, beautifully dressed in long dresses of precious fabrics, crouched down on their heels, according to Japanese custom. They remained straight and still, their eyes tied to the grid that separated us from them, and having in their bright eyes, that particular fixity of those who do not realize what they see. Their beautiful jet-black hair was artistically arranged and adorned with long yellow flakes pins. They were in their early youth, the oldest was barely twenty years old, the youngest were just over fourteen years old. Some of them were noticed for their beauty, but all of them had a resigned, tired, indifferent look, especially, which did not fit well with their young faces, and which was painful to see. Displayed as are the curious animals in a menagerie, examined and criticized at leisure by each curious person, to be sold or rented to the first bidder, these unfortunate women presented a show that caused me the most painful impression. An old woman appeared at the entrance to the room and said a few words; one of the girls immediately got up, but with the slowness of an automaton. There was, in this way of moving, something unconscious as in trained animals, which perform, on the order of their master, some of the maneuvers they are used to. »

of arms.

And it is still the toilet of the woman in these houses, combing her hair, putting make-up on, blackening her teeth.

But here we are at the very bottom of prostitution, where the brush of a Japanese painter rarely comes down. On the door of a tea house, courtesans look, as if with disgusted curiosity, at hideous old women, covered with rags, ancestors hanging up in the street, near the wooden warehouses, and indulging in the manner of our stoners, in the open air, next to dogs mounted one on top of the other.

In this series, let us mention a board that has a great character in this land of water: it is the low prostitution of the river and the river, depicted in the night of heaven, in the night of the landscape, in the night of dead water, by a long black woman with bare feet, a woman immobilized straight, and which stands out, in darkness, on the whiteness of a boat with a cane roof.

In this book on the Yoshiwara, Toyokouni, often Outamaro's equal in his triptychs, is beaten by his rival. His women do not have the elegance of body, the grace bypassed by movements, the physical aristocracy of the Japanese prostitute. Even there is not, among his images, the spirit of drawing, the life of composition, the surprise of nothing of the voluptuousness of the local woman. Then the comic note, which Toyokouni seems to prefer, in the representation of the scenes of the Yoshiwara, adds triviality to the common work. Moreover, to judge the talent of the two emulated painters, one only has to compare the Outamaro Women's Exhibition and the Toyokouni Women's Exhibition: the former is a small wonder, the latter is a very, very ordinary board.

XVII

The Japanese woman is small, small, small, small and plump. Of this woman, Outamaro has made her the slender woman, the woman slender of her impressions: a woman who has the lengths of *thoughts,* Watteau's pre-midday pictures. Perhaps, before Outamaro, Kiyonaga had done it like him, larger than life, but fleshy and thick.

The Japanese woman's face is short, compact, it has a little of the flattening of our cheap masks, and a little bit in the features of the denting of these pieces of cardboard; finally this face, except the untranslatable soft vivacity of the black eyes, it is such in its round shape, that we represent it Harunobou, Koriusai, Shunshô.

Well, from that face, Outamaro made an almost long oval! And perhaps in the hieratic drawing of the human figure in Nippon, which condemns the painter to reproduce the eyes only through two slits with a small dot in the middle, the nose only through a line of aquiline calligraphy, and the same for all the noses of the Sunrise Empire, In the mouth, that by two small things, resembling petals curled up in flowers, Outamaro is the first one who has slipped into these faces, from a convention so little human, a mutinous grace, a naive surprise, a spiritual understanding, - and the first, who, while preserving the consecrated lines and forms, but bringing them almost invisibly to human lines and forms, in certain plates of the beautiful weather of his talent, puts around these lines so many things of the life of real portraits, that when you look at these figures, you hardly notice any more the hieratic nature of this face, of this universal face, which has become by miracle, in Outamaro, a particular physiognomy for each human being, represented in its images.

Finally, the woman, in the ungrateful way of reproducing her, imposed on the artist by the art of her country, Outamaro strives and succeeds in embellishing her, in making her elegant, let us say the word, in idealizing her. Because Outamaro is an idealist painter of the woman, but a particular painter, an idealist painter of his type, his physique, his anatomical construction, but while remaining the most *naturist* painter of his attitudes, his movements, the mimic of his gracious humanity.

And since Outamaro's studies are almost always focused on the woman of the "Green Houses", it is the courtesan he idealizes, and whose, according to the expression of a Japanese man, - and the expression is to be noted, - he *makes a goddess*

XVIII

The strange, the unbelievable, the incredible in this draftsman, this idealistic draftsman of women, is that, when he wants to, he becomes the most exact, rigorous, photographic draftsman, of the bird, the reptile, the shell, yes, the very small shell; he is, when he wants to, the most concerned illustrator at the same time as the most artistic in natural history that exists. And the reproduction of these beings and these things of nature, we must see them in these three books with the title:

Yehon Momotidori. THE HUNDRED CRIERS (birds).

Yehon Moushi Yerabi. SELECTED INSECTS.

Shiohi-no-tsuto. MEMORIES OF THE LOW TIDE.

Ah! these are drawings other than the famous vellums of our famous Natural History Cabinet, and drawings reproduced by color prints, like no country in Europe has yet managed to print them.

In *Yehon Momotidori,* THE HUNDRED SCREAMERS, THE

charming impression that the "pickling doves" in its appearance of a fine pen drawing, simply washed with blue water. What an admirable impression it gives to this duck which, thanks to a slight relief, seems to be painted in watercolor on its plumage, a little raised. But what a marvel this other impression, representing "cranes and a kingfisher hunting", cranes which are, so to speak, in their characteristic silhouette, in their clever construction, only a white embossing, and this semi-submerged kingfisher whose half of body plunges into the river is a wonder of the rendering of the fading beyond color and the blurring of the shape under water.

In *Yehon Moushi Yerabi*, CHOSEN INSECTS, quite extraordinary boards like the games of a frog in a water lily leaf, like the pursuit of a lizard by a snake: and in all these impressions, the astonishing detachment of the caterpillar, the grasshopper, the kite on the softness of the green of the leaves, on the softness of the pink of the flowers, and again in these impressions the trompe-l'oeil of the green bronze of the corselet of the beetles, the diamond and *emerald* gauze of the wings of the dragonflies, finally, the introduction so learned, so clever in the coloration of insects, the brilliants and the metallic reflections, that light makes appear on them.

But apart from the miraculous perfection of the color impressions of this book, it is of particular interest to the French writer studying the artist's talent, because it contains at the head of this volume a preface written by Toriyama Sékiyen, the master of Outamaro, celebrating the *naturism* (out of the heart) of his little one, his dear student *Outa*.

And here is this preface, for which I owe the translation and translation of the text of Jipensha Ikkou's Green Houses, to the intelligent, the learned, the kind Mr. Hayashi, and, it must be said highly, to whom all Japanese people today owe all the documentary interest of their work.

"*Reproducing life through the heart, and drawing its structure with a brush, is the law of painting. The study that my student Outamaro has just published now reproduces the very life of the insect world. This is the real painting of the heart. And when I remember the past, I remember that from childhood the little* Outa *observed the smallest detail of things. So, in the fall, when he was in the garden, he would hunt insects, and whether it was a cricket or a grasshopper, he had made a catch, he kept the bug in his hand, and had fun studying it. And how many times I scolded him, in the apprehension that he would get into the habit of killing living beings.*

Now that he has acquired his great talent as a brush, he has made these insect studies the glory of his profession. Yes, he manages to make the shine of the tamanushi (insect name) *sing, in order to shake the old paint, and he borrows the small arms of the grasshopper to make war with it, and he uses the capacity of the earthworm, to dig the ground, under the base of the old building. He tries to penetrate the mystery of nature with the trial and error of the larvae, by lighting his way with the firefly, and he ends up managing, by grabbing the end of the thread from the spider's web. He had faith in the publication of the Masters' kiôka; as for the merit of the engraving* (of the wooden carving), *it is the work of Fouji Kazumouné's chisel.*

The winter of the 7th year of Temmei (1787).

Toriyama Sékiyen[40].

We can clearly see that this preface is a revolutionary manifesto of

---

[40] You can read on the black stamp: *Toriyama,* and on the white *Toyofousa.* We will notice that Sékiyen used to call Outamaro, *Oula* in short.

the profane school, the *vulgar school* (called Oukiyo-yé) against the old painting of the Buddhist schools of Kano, Tosa.

XX

However, of all these books of natural artistic history, the most exquisite is *Shiohi-no-tsuto*, MEMORIES OF THE LOW TIDE, *poems on shells by members of a literary society.*

A first plate shows you women and children looking for shells on a beach, from which the sea has receded, and it is after a series of plates printed in color, making it impossible to color the shells with diffuse spots of precious stones, these mother-of-pearl shells, these *black pearled* burgau shells, of these shells with *radiated ruby eyes*, making there, really on the paper, the microscopic accident of these shells, to the *bites of flies, of* these ribbed, flaked, lamellar, tubular, vermicular shells, of these shells curled in *sea cabbage,* or needled with prickles, like the backs of hedgehogs.

And the book ends with a board, representing the game of *kai-awassé, a* special game for young Japanese women, which we see crouching down, in a pretty interior, around a shell circle.

XXI

Outamaro is not only looked upon in Japan, as the founder of THE SCHOOL OF LIFE, is not only considered as an admirable designer

of birds, fish, insects, he is admired as one of the great masters of
SPRING PAINTING: painting which, in Japan, does not only mean
painting of the renewal of the earth, but what we call in Europe "light
painting".

I have a rare album, dated 1790, and having as its title: *Foughen-zô*
or WALKS AT THE TIME OF THE FLOWERING OF CHERRY
BLOSSOMS[41], which gives the idea of celtic painting, by putting
in the flowering of flowering trees of the province of Yoshino-Yama,
pretty walkers.

---

[41] There is no more sincerely national taste, says Mr. Bousquet, in JAPAN
TODAY than the Japanese people's penchant for nature scenes, their love of
vegetation and flowers. Not only do the rich surround their homes with
plantations, but it is not so modest, whose threshold or courtyard does not contain
any shrubs, and whose interior is not brightened by a vase of flowers... In spring,
we will see the blooming of the *mummy* plum trees in Mumeyaski, Tokaido; a
little later, in April, we go in crowds to Muko-Sima, Ileno, Oji, to admire the pink
snow falling from the cherry trees, forming a wonderful contrast with the dark
greenery of the fir trees that surround them. From morning to evening, these
gardens are filled with walkers of all ages and conditions, to whom small bamboo
huts, decorated with paper lanterns, provide temporary shelter. Cakes, tea, cherry
blossom infusions are served. They sell toys there. Young girls play music there,
and everything inspires happiness, carefree and cheerfulness. In June, comes the
turn of the *fudsi,* wisteria. Picnics are being organized. The poets deploy their
verve and go and stain a madrigal on the branches of the tree that sheltered them.
Shortly afterwards, it is still on the edge of its river that the people of Yédo will
admire the irises, which grow in considerable quantities, varied in color and
appearance, in the middle of the neighbouring marshes. Finally, in autumn, the
chrysanthemum *kiku is the* favourite flower. The gardens, where it is grown, are
full until the frost comes to kill the flowers, and confine the Japanese to their
homes

To this series are linked the albums: *Yehon Waka-yébisu,* JAPANESE POEMS OF THE FIRST DAY OF THE YEAR, *Yehon Gnin-sékai,* POEMS ON THE SNOW; *Yehon Kiôghètsubô,* POEMS ON THE MOON.

XXII

Outamaro has in his work all kinds of compositions, and compositions where the artist's imagination shows great ingenuity.

I will mention, for example, the series of the *Four Donors*, in which Outamaro, giving in the small image of the bottom of the board, the reproduction of an old master's drawing, makes, so to speak, a spiritual parody of the consecrated work through a large scene of its composition, a scene that is not unrelated to the scenes of ancient history, interpreted by Daumier's powerful food pencil.

I will quote again this series or, unlike Grandville seeking human silhouettes for animals, Outamaro gives men, thanks to its learned avoidance of animals, gives by circumvention and deformation, a disturbing similarity with certain animals[42].

Finally, I would like to mention, in a completely different order, this

---

[42] And the painter is served, helped in these metamorphoses, by one of the most primitive clothing, as described by M. Remy in his MEDICAL NOTES ON JAPAN: straw sandals on his feet, bare lower limbs, a white towel between his legs and attached to his belt, a jacket with wide sleeves open at the front, a hemispherical hat on his head against the sun, a blue handkerchief to wipe his face: this is the Japanese people's entire clothing, when he is not only wearing tattoos.

series in which we see, at the top of each board, a pair of glasses, one of which bears: *Eyes of parents,* and the other: *Teachings,* and whose true translation is: *Parents' councils,* - and which seem to be a series of small actions of private life, done as if under the command of these old eyes, and to the effect of satisfying and delighting them[43].

XXIII

Sometimes Outamaro abandons the representation of real life, and lets himself go to charming imaginations in the chimera. We know of him a series of a dozen boards, entitled: GOOD DREAMS: *it is as much a win,* where behind the head of the man or woman who sleeps, he shows, in the distance of the board, he shows in action, the dream they have.

A dream that comes out of their minds, not from their brains, but from their chests, and a little like a phylactery coming out of the mouths of our saints, and which, in the Japanese image, extends and widens in the shape of a kite.

We see the sleep of a little girl evoking an exquisite dinner, which she eats *gourmetly*; we see the sleep of a charming young girl, whose

---

[43] There is even ingenuity in Outamaro, not only in the invention of subjects, but in doing so. Thus, ARTISTIC JAPAN gave a servant of a tea house, a servant whom the legend of the image teaches us to serve in the *Maniba* house, and who, in the original on a sheet of paper, thin as an onion skin, and where we see it both from the front and the back, is printed with such accuracy of location, that the sheet, crossed by light, allows only one character to be seen.

face shines through the screen folded over her eyes, and who dreams that she has become a princess, whose norimon crosses the countryside under the escort of a large troop of women of company and service; we see the sleep of a courtesan from Yoshiwara, transporting her to a small interior, where the prostitute out of prostitution, indulges with the beloved man, in the care of the household; we see the sleep of an old samurai servant, reviving him in good weather, where he was hanging up in the street, by a hooded little girl.

And in this humorous series, there are not only the dreams of human beings, there are the dreams of animals; and we witness the sleep of an old cat, dreaming of the alert and thieving days of his young age, where he devoured the fish prepared for his master's meal, despite his efforts to pull it out of his mouth, despite the enormous bamboo brought by the woman to beat him.

XXIV

Outamaro was the most popular.

At the beginning of this century, a traveler from the province of Ivaki, who was continuously running in the northern region for his business, and who happened to be, at the same time, a passionate amateur of engravings, visiting collectors in the cities where he passed, this traveler affirmed that in all the provinces of Japan, Outamaro was considered as the greatest master of the Empire, while Toyokouni was very little known.

Myself, in the images, I discover a curious testimony of this popularity: it is a sourimono, having all the characters of the teacher's drawing, and which is certainly one of his students. However, this sourimono represents a large pleasure boat, whose cabin is filled with women, women with elegant figuration whose brush the artist worked on throughout his life: a boat bearing in large characters Outamaro, *the boat Outamaro*[44].

In support of this account of the Japanese traveler, and the image of the ship Outamaro, we can count that in the last years of Outamaro's life, his studio was, all day long, besieged by publishers placing orders with him, absolutely as if there was no other artist but him in Japan.

Outamaro's talent was even appreciated in China, where merchant ships arriving in Nagasaki bought, in large numbers, his color prints.

XXV

Among the contemporary painters, apart from Toyokouni, who was Outamaro's rival and competitor, and who, in his compositions, had the same objective of grace, there is another master, with whom Outamaro sometimes has the greatest kinship, and in whose impressions it is sometimes necessary, for the best connoisseur of Japanese prints, to seek the signature, to be sure that the image is not of the founder of THE SCHOOL OF LIFE. Do I need to name Yeishi, whose women of a more ingenious, more mystical, we can even say more religious, finally, more women of our medieval miniatures, have the slender lengths, the frail little necks, the thin forearms, at the same time as the Eastern nonchalance of the key attitudes of the Outamaro women's movements.

---

[44] The name was made easier by the end of the name used in Japan by all the boats, which is *Maro*.

There is still a greater resemblance between the two painters, it is that only the two of them, in the coloring of their *Nishiki-yes,* have published colored plates, as well as the " Walk of the little daimio, a sparrow on his hand ", have published plates whose harmonic charm is obtained by the only use on a yellowish background, blue, green, violet, with, in these three colors, the black of a dress or a belt: - a charm that is both sweet and severe, a half-mourning charm.

XXVI

In his compositions, Outamaro sometimes referred to the men of power at the end of a spiritually allusive brush. Didn't I mention in a series on Taikô, the winning hero of the Koreans, the popular man of the late sixteenth century, a board, where he is depicted courting a young lord, whose coat of arms is very recognizable on his sleeve. Is it a young lord from the time of Taikô Hideyoshï ?

Finally, it was wrong for the painter to touch politics the last time he did, when he published the plate with the legend: THE PLEASURES OF TAÏKÔ WITH ITS FIVE WOMEN IN THE EAST OF THE CAPITAL; a triptych board representing the hero with the monkey head[45] giving back the sake bowl he has just emptied, at the moment when a kneeling man presents him his official hairstyle, the *kammuri, the* hairstyle of the highest title, and that under the trees in bloom, in the perimeter of a silk curtain, where his coat of arms is repeated in purple, advances with a queen's port towards the illustrious warrior, surrounded by women, the

---

[45] A curious wooden statuette of General Sarou. "of the monkey general", was reproduced in the 34th issue of Japan Artistic.

legitimate wife, holding in her hand a closed fan, and on her hair untied and spread on her shoulders, wearing as hairstyle, two large clumps of chrysanthemums in gold and silver.

This seemingly innocent impression would be a reminder of the end of the famous Taiko, who fell to the decline of his life in libertine and the dissolution of morals, a bloody reminder to Iyenari, bearing the honorary name of Dun-kiô-in, the eleventh shogun of the Tokugawa family, the shogun who reigned in the last years of Outamaro's existence, and who, it seems, was a kind of voluptuous Louis XV and an art lover, as was the French monarch.

Outamaro was sentenced to prison by the authorities of Yédo, from which he took his weakened and sick body out.

XXVII

Long before he knew that Outamaro was a kind of official painter of the Yoshiwara, one day, while leafing through, with Hayaski, his TWELVE HOURS suite, in front of the sixth plate, representing this gracefully woman, dressed in a pale dress, starred with drawings such as starfish, with a faded azure and as if drowned in water, this woman, to whom a *mousmé* (girl) presents, kneeling, a cup of tea, and whose frail neck, a shoulder top voluptuously thin with phtisique, a small pointed breast, emerge from the falling fabric, I said to Hayashi:

—— The man who drew this woman must have been a lover of the woman's body ?

—— You said it, Hayashi answered me, he died of exhaustion.

Indeed, Outamaro died in his house on the bridge of Beneï, from the abuse of pleasure, and a little of his stay in prison, and again, after leaving prison, from his unremitting and restless work, to satisfy all the late orders, and the new orders arriving every day.

XXVIII

Every Japanese painter has an erotic work, his *shungwa* (spring paintings). The painter of the Green Houses, with his talent belonging to the great prostitute, to the rich venal love, could not fail to have, in his immense production, his free work, images à la Jules Romain, a *hell* in bibliographic style.

But really, the erotic painting of this people is to be studied for the fanatics of drawing, by the ardor, the fury of these copulations, as if angered; by the tumbling of these ruts overturning the screens of a room; by the entanglements of the bodies fused together; by the women enjoy of arms at the same time, attracting and repelling the coitus; by the epilepsy of those feet with twisted toes, beating the air; by those devouring mouth-to-mouth kisses; by those woman's palms, her head knocked down, with the *little death* on their faces, with closed eyes, under their wraparound eyelids, - finally by this force, this power of the lineature, which makes the drawing of a rod, a drawing equal to the hand of the Louvre Museum, attributed to Michelangelo.

Then, what! in the midst of these animal frenzies of the flesh, tasty collections of the being, blissful collapses, neck-breaks of our primitive painters, mystical attitudes, almost religious movements of love.

Sometimes in these erotic compositions, funny eccentric imaginations, like this sketch, showing the luxurious dream of a woman, having rejected her blankets far from her body in heat, and who sees a farandole of phallus, swaying and dancing under Japanese dresses, venting with huge fans: a completely original composition, taken from an artist's brain and brush, in an hour of libertine caprice.

Sometimes terrible boards, boards that are a little scary. Thus on rocks green with seaweeds, a naked body of a woman, a naked body of a woman vanished clans of pleasure, *sicut cadaver*, to such an extent that one does not know whether it is a drowned or a living one, and of which an immense octopus, with its frightening black moon-shaped sloes, sucks in the bottom of the body, while a small octopus goulashes its mouth.

And again, in this strange book entitled: *Yehon-Kimmo-Zuyé*. THE ILLUSTRATED ENCYCLOPEDIA FOR YOUNG PEOPLE, whose drawings are somewhat related to the books of writers with deranged imaginations, extravagant concepts, slightly crazy books or, according to Montaigne, "the spirit, making the escaped horse the child of chimeras", in this astronomical, astrological, physiological and heterogeneous collection, they are a kind of philosopho-pornographic rebus where the sexuality of humans changes into maps of the sky and the earth, where the men's minnows (sea leeches) transform into fantastic men of unknown planets, where the natural parts of women sometimes become an apocalyptic bird of prey, sometimes a landscape where the Fuzi-Yama can be recognized.

Outamaro has therefore imagined it from a certain number of albums in black and color, where the qualities of the designer are found, but where the naked of his naked courtesans no longer has, for me, the grace they shake and stir in their long and enveloping dresses.

However, there are some compositions worthy of the master. In the book entitled: THE FIRST ESSAY ON WOMEN, it is a charming drawing: the drawing of a woman, the arms passed, the arms passed from afar around the neck of her lover, and her head in a dove love bending, fallen against the chest of the man she caresses with her neck, while the bottom of both bodies is welded in sexual rapprochement.

In A THOUSAND KINDS OF COLORS, it is a fun board. It is a woman dropping her lantern, at the sight of four feet coming out of a blanket, four feet, two of them very hairy, with about this legend in the woman's mouth: "*How can four feet in the bed of only one person!* »

A dreadful board of Outamaro as a representation of Lust, shows us a monster, a huge man with pale flesh, bloodless, all strewn with hair corkscrews, his mouth hideously distorted by the spasm of pleasure, wallowing, flattened on a young woman's delicate and slender body: a board where in the physical jouissance of a human being, certainly the draftsman sought to make the jouissance of the toad, by a serial souvenir, where the small fan placed at the top of each board indicates an imitation of an animal by a man, and where by the attitudes and the gesticulation, it is in a board almost the transformation from a man to a toad.

This plate is part of a color album entitled: THE POEM OF THE PILLOW, a marvel of impression, of a harmony of which, I repeat, no European impression is approaching, and where the clarity of naked bodies is so brightly removed from the colors of silk clothes, scattered under the lovemaking, and where the fawn spot of the Venus mountains stands out so voluptuously on the barely pink whiteness of the female skin.

The first plate of the collection is an original composition. This Outamaro, who in his fantastic series and quite inferior to Hokusai, and who has nothing like the five terrifying heads of this master, has the fantastic in eroticism. And here is what this board represents: a marine deity, raped underwater by amphibious monsters in the midst of the curiosity of small fish trying to slip in with the monsters, while squatting on the shore of an islet, a young girl, a half-naked fisherman, looks at the strange and troubled spectacle of the abyss, all soft, all open to temptation.

XXIX

Outamaro died in Yédo, in 1806, on the third day of the fifth month of the lunar calendar[46]. In the old copies of Oukiyo-yé Bouikô, the date of Outamaro's death is falsely given, as it occurred on the eighth day of the twelfth month of Kwansei's fourth year, which is the year 1792. However, since THE YOSHIWARA YEARBOOK was published in 1804, and the plate representing a "Japanese Olympus" being dated: *On the day of* 1805, the real date of Outamaro's death is later: it is the date of 1806, given in a copy of a more recent date, owned by a Tokio

---

[46] The Japanese year is twelve months old, like ours. The first month in the poetic language, and in the language spoken at the court of the Mikado, is called the *friendly month, because of the* good friendship that is assumed, generated by the gifts and visits of New Year's Day. The name of the second month is the month when *you double your clothes, and it is the* time of the great cold. The third month is the month of *resurrection* or the beginning of spring, very early in these latitudes. The fourth month, the month of *deutzia, a* flower resembling jasmine. Then come the months of *drought,* the month of *missives,* because, according to the old custom, letters of congratulations were written to each other; then the months of *falling leaves,* with *long clarity,* the *month without god, the month without god,* where the divinity of thunder is supposed to die, without being replaced by another, the month of *white frost,* and finally the month of the *race of the masters, which in the* last days of the year, under the influence of business to be finished, are always by ways and paths.

amateur, who kindly made a copy for Hayashi, during his last trip to Japan.

XXX

The portrait, as we execute it in Europe, the portrait representing the exact features, the rigorous lineaments, the particularities of a figure, is not made in Japan, - except perhaps, quite exceptionally, the portrait of some priest or some monk. There is therefore no need to expect to encounter a portrait, engraved or drawn, of a Japanese artist's face. Fortunately, the painters from there sometimes had the fantasy of leaving them, not an image of their face, but a silhouette of their person. Thus, the tradition makes two or three boards of Hokusai, figurations of the master.

For the representation of Outamaro, we have better than problematic boards, we have the second impression of the series of PAINTINGS OF FORTY-SEVEN RONINS *represented by the most beautiful women*, which shows us, in the night of a garden of the Yoshiwara, a man in the middle of courtesans giving, an empty cup of sake, to a woman bent over him. And on the pilaster, at the foot of which the man is sitting, is engraved: "*On request, Outamaro painted his elegant face himself.* »

The registration does not lie. If it is not the face, whose design still has the hieratic quality of album figures, it is the man who is elegant, and full of a coquettish search for the care of his hair, so well lifted on the top of his head, so well combed on the faces, in the theatrical attitude with which he seems to pose on the ground, in the sober distinction of her costume, her upper dress, this black dress all sown with little white peas, which make her look like a guinea fowl's feathers, - and at the top of her chest, can be read in two small circles of yellow silk, on one side, *Outa,* and on the other, *Maro.*

Here we are talking about a plate from this erotic book entitled: THE PILLOW POEM (1788) which shows Outamaro, moved from the garden into the house, and into a much greater intimacy with a local creature.

It is a large composition in width in which, in front of an open terrace bay, where the green stem of a shrub rises, lies on a bench, a man whose face faces, is hidden by a woman seen from behind, kissing her on the mouth, and letting see from the man's face only a little thwarted and a piece of chin, which his hand has taken, and around which she turns in a passionate grip.

In this erotic composition, there is in the arrangement, the drawing, the color, as an art in love with the reproduction of the woman, her abundant hair, her frail neck, her dark-colored dress, sown with small light bouquets, made of intertwined hatches, and also as an art in love with the reproduction of the man, its soft pose, its elegant sensuality, its voluptuous laziness, the interruption of the path and the coming and going of its fan, bringing the little allusive poetry to the artist's situation, compared to the beak of the crane, which we often see in netzkés caught in a bivalve shell: "The *beak strongly pinched by the amajouri* (shell), *the bird can no longer fly away*", - and a grey fan like its dress, the dress imitating a guinea fowl plumage, which it already wears, in its authentic portrait, in the last of the PAINTINGS OF THE FORTY-SEVEN RONINS, *formed by the most beautiful women,* and which makes it quite famous to me.

Yes, the plate is not signed, does not bear anything that indicates the artist's personality, and yet this something intuitive, revealing, this something inexplicable, experienced at first sight of this print, and of which we cannot give the explanation by words or sentences, tells me that : it is painted by Outamaro himself, a second portrait of Outamaro, in intimate conversation with a beloved courtesan of Yoshiwara, perhaps the woman so often reproduced by her brush, the beautiful Kisegawa - and everything confirms to me in this presumption, even the anonymity, in this indiscreet plate, of the artist's figure, hidden by a woman's kiss.

XXXI

Outamaro died, his widow remarried one of her students, Koïkawa-Shuntiô, who took the name Outamaro, and who continued, under that name, to execute the orders made to the deceased. Later, in the Work of Outamaro, a good number of impressions bearing the signature of the Master, with banal composition, heads without expression, inharmonic colors.

And we do not have to rely only on the impressions of the widow's husband, not only on the forgeries that occurred in the midst of the artist's great popularity, and forced him, for a moment, as I have already said, to sign his plates: *the real Outamaro,* but we must still reject, I believe, a number of his plates, made in his workshop by his students Kikumaro, Hidémaro, Takimaro, and others, that he let them sign with his name.

It even happens that this artist of a very personal talent, at the beginning of his career, allowed Kiyonaga to exercise such a domination of his work, and towards the end of his career, sometimes let himself go to look so much like Heishi, that collectors, in this dissemblance and inferiority of a certain number of impressions, where they do not find the beautiful maturity beyond powerful youth, the artist's healthy originality, wonder in the days of skepticism that collectors sometimes have, if there have not been several Outamaro.

XXXII

According to some Kakemonos (in Japanese: *the thing you hang*), arrived in Europe, according to the water coloring of about ten strips of paper or gauze, the only painting known in Japan, we can appreciate, we can judge the painting of Outamaro.

This painting has the soft clarity, the harmony of the tones faded from its impressions, at the same time as the boldness of a first touch quite remarkable, and that only partially gives us the impression in color.

In my collection, there is a Japanese woman, seen from behind, represented with this movement in the march, from the belly forward, a movement usual to the woman from there, and supporting with a hand that we do not see, the heavy fallout of her dress and her raised belt.

A pochade in India ink, on a paper that drinks, and executed with fury, anger, anger, that a European artist only sometimes puts to his shooting. Black crushed with brushes mixed, with two or three scarlets of vermilion, resembling blood underneath, and where one can see, in the artist's smear, at the bottom of the tail of the dress, roofs of temples crowning cryptomerias lines, and at the top, a frail woman's neck with small twisted hair, above which a hairstyle spreads, looking like a large butterfly, with open wings.

Another kakemono of the same family, and of similar *origin*, is a kakemono belonging to Mr. Hayashi. She is a dancer mimicking a dance of character, an ancient noble dance, under the archaic dress of this dance.

She is wearing the little teddy bear-shaped cap, *yeboshi* tied to her hair on her shoulders, by a cord tied under her chin, and the dancer moving and developing in the wide dress, holds with both hands, lowered against her hip, the *uchiwa* fan.

Another pochade removed with Indian ink, on a slightly dark paper, where there is only a reddish tint on the dress, and the carmine of the attachment of her hat and acorns of her belt.

A very superior kakemono is the one from Outamaro, which Mr. Bing exhibited at the Beaux-Arts.

It depicts, in a graceful contour of the body, an endearing woman, with both arms raised in the air, a mosquito net, above a child, lying with her back on the ground, her legs in the air: On the pretty grey tone of the Chinese paper of the composition, the green of the mosquito net stands out, a little red of the naked child's apron, the powerful black of the woman's belt, a lacquered belt, where shiny fern branches are removed on the mat of the fabric's bottom. It is of an extraordinary effect, this opposition of three tones in this greyness.

Another kakemono from my collection shows you a Japanese woman unrolling a poem. She has this white gouache figure, which gives almost all women kakemonos, the Pierrot appearance, and is dressed in a rust colored dress with white flower stems at the bottom, and a black belt, crossed by stripes of young birds, in the red yellow of the dress. Always as in Mr. Bing's kakemono, the opposition of a lacquer black with shades washed out with plenty of water.

Finally, when my work is finished, I am shown, at Bing's, a huge kakemono, a kakemono three meters wide and 50 centimeters wide and two meters 40 centimeters high, a kakemono filling an entire one-piece panel, and on which is represented a composition, in which there are twenty-six women. It is the perspective of a turn in the inner gallery of a "Green House" above a garden with snow-covered shrubs, where they are grouped and nicely layered into lazy stops, or into quick stair climbs, these courtesans, barefoot, under their sumptuous dresses: women playing with a small dog, women carrying a snack, women talking from top to bottom of the stairs, leaning down the ramps with eloquent hand gestures, women thinking distractedly, an arm surrounding the wooden pilaster against which they are leaning standing, women making music, women, frightfully squatting around a brazier, on which a teapot ends, - and in the background, a woman passing, carrying on her back, in a green bag, bedding objects.

A composition where the types, attitudes and grace of Outamaro's gestures are found, but in a quick process, a little grossly decorative, without clarity in the water coloring; a composition not signed, but which by its origin would undoubtedly be the master's, and this is what its history would be. Under the influence of one of the many apprehensions of imprisonment, allegedly experienced by Outamaro, following the publication of a satirical plate, the artist hid for some time with a friend in a remote province, and this immense kakemono would have been a thank you for the hospitality he had received.

XXXIII

Outamaro, we saw him, during his lifetime, having a large number of imitators in his way, whether they were trained at his school or elsewhere; after his death it is even larger, and among them appears in the first line the new husband of the deceased's wife. But they are low imitators, plagiarists. Outamaro basically has only one student who has continued with personal qualities. This student is Shikimaro.

Certainly, in his book entitled: *Zensei Tagû-no-Kurabé*, a MEETING OF WOMEN IN GREAT BLOSSOMING OF BEAUTY, women, however long they may be, in the amplitude, the engulfment, the undulation of dresses, in the crushing sumptuousness of the stars, in the overload of drawings and embroideries, no longer have the slender distinction of the women of Outamaro; they take a little too much of the massiveness of the *portentosa* epithet, given by the Latins to their material goddesses, at the same time as their grace is more twisted, more contorted, let us say, more theatrical.

Then again, it is no longer the discreet harmony of the master's colors. There is no longer in these impressions, the transparencies and subtleties of the impressions of Outamaro and his contemporaries - it is finally over with what, I don't know what, which takes away their wallpaper appearance, that modern impressions will have.

XXXIV

Ah! the beautiful impressions of the end of the eighteenth century and the very first beginning of the nineteenth ! Ah ! the beautiful impressions of Outamaro, which have for the eyes of the taste lover, the seductive charm of the *art print*[47]. Yes, those impressions that seem to

---

[47] Here is a question. Should the beauty of these impressions be placed entirely on the painter's account, and should it not be taken into account by the engraver, as it seems to happen in Japan, where the engraver's name does not usually sign, rarely reaches the public. Well, I'd believe it enough. There the

have lost nothing to the mechanically industrial popularization that popularizes them, and that seem to have remained, in their interpretation by the printer, the master's drawings, - impressions that have kept the clarity, the clarity, the watercolor watercolor !

Oh, when you put them next to modern impressions, what a contrast between their harmonious greens, their harmonious blues, their harmonious reds, their harmonious yellows, their harmonious violets, with the greens that hurt the eyes, the hard blues, the black reds, the ugly ochre yellows, the cotton violets! What a contrast between their transparency, and the matte tone, without depth, of these images whose rough colors seem to be made with cheap colored powders.

Let us look at Mr. Gonse's proof of the dragonfly in poppies, of the book of SELECTED INSECTS, - not the proof of the book, which is already very beautiful in early editions, - but a proof of the very first printing, a test proof perhaps, it is not printing, it is a drawing with all the finesse, lightness, the *human hand* side of a real drawing, of

---

engraver seems to me to be absolutely only the painter's worker, and always work under his inspiration, and even have talent only under his eye. I would see in this surveillance of the printer, reasons for Outamaro's lifelong residence with his publisher, where the engraving workshop was located. And indeed, the proof of what I am saying is when the painter is dead, or when the engraver no longer fires under his supervision, the print is no longer the same. - Yes, in Japan, the drawing is not the mechanical drawing of our European shooter: each drawing in this unhurried work of the pressed order, is the attempt to achieve a better success, the effort towards obtaining something not obtained until then, the satisfaction that the worker gives himself, to make come out from under the wood, an image other than the previous one; a more perfect image, an image, an image, so to speak new.

something not reproduced in several copies.

That next to it, we look at this plate representing two women and a little girl, at the entrance of a bridge, it's not really an impression yet, it's a watercolor where the delicate relief of the embroidery enhanced with a little gold does so well, because embossing, this decor in our country of confectioners, they have made it an art accessory in their impressions; and that we look, in M. Gillot, all these surprising proofs, where there is such a soft fading of color, such a tender diffusion of tones, that they appear to you, as well as the colorings of a watercolor bathing for a moment in water, or rather, as well as the softly luminous colorings of the miniatures of children, thrown in the state of a sketch by Fragonard, on the fat of an ivory leaf.

But in this enormous, incredible number of admirable impressions, let's talk for a moment about these series at the bottom of silver, with the mirrors, in front of which women wash, these mirrors with the frame, and the small easel, lacquered in real lacquer. Let us talk about these impressions, about the thousand details of a precious execution, about the rendering by a thousand small strokes, about the teeming birth of hair, on the temples and on the forehead, - about hair that is in modern impressions only a confused, muddy mass[48], about these impressions or, in the silvering of the background, putting on these images like a white lunar reflection, the women, in their discreet coloring, have pink tea flesh, and appear in turquoise blue, redcurrant pink, yellow gold green dresses, finally dressed in colors of tenderness, which I have not met on a colored print of any country.

Moreover, background have always been a major concern at

---

[48] It is above all the finesse and sharpness of the work of wood engraving in the hair that makes it possible to recognize, at first sight, the good proofs.

Outamaro. He never agreed to give his women, as a background, the raw whiteness of the paper, removing them sometimes on a straw yellow or orange hue, whose uniformity he broke by small clouds of micaceous dust, both black and shiny, sometimes on a grey hue having something in his work of trampling the sea, on a beach that she had left. Rather than leaving them white, his backgrounds, he will make them cross the undulation of a wave of violet or tobacco. Sometimes, as well as in the series we have just mentioned, its backgrounds around the figures will show like the drooling silver of a snail's passage, produced by silver or by silver white made with bleak. Sometimes his backgrounds will have an appearance of oxidized metal, reminiscent of the backgrounds of his predecessor Shirakou: - strange, strange, surprising backgrounds, with their bold colorings on the metal, backgrounds on which, it really seems that in these paper images, the painter wanted the multicolored patina of Japanese bronzes. Finally, one would think, this search for what can damage a bottom has been so great, so ingenious, at Outamaro, that in a choice test, the "Hot bath given by a mother to her child", the bottom of the board is artistically dusted with crushed coal, with which we heat a bath.

In this study of beautiful impressions, Mr. Gillot's collection offers us the most instructive elements of comparison, by combining several different states of the same composition. For example, for the "CLEANING OF THE MORNING OF A GREEN HOUSE, AT THE END OF THE YEAR", there are three different states of coloring: a first state, where in the lineature of the finest contours, it is an assemblage of faded shades, and almost entirely held in greenish, yellowish tones; a second state, where it is perceived as the introduction of suspicions of blue and violet tones; a third state in its natural colors, always harmonious, but of a less distinguished polychromy.

Another most curious impression is the impression of "THE

PRINCESS DESCENDED FROM HER IMPERIAL CHARIOT, AND WALKING IN THE COUNTRYSIDE", WHICH is an impression in the ordinary state where purple dominates and which, in this first state of coloration, seems to be an attempt by the printer, to give the sensation of a plate to the print made with gold, and where all tones are yellow or a yellowish bister, in the middle of which stand out the beautiful black of the lacquered wheels of the Imperial chariot.

Results at the bottom obtained by technical means by the thickness of soft paper, where the coloring is not only on the surface, but has penetrated, has crossed the paper, so that the bulk of the coloring is drunk and retained in the interior, and that it appears from it only the transparency through the silk[49] of Japanese paper, like a tone under a glaze.

But that is not enough, there is in these impressions a decomposition of color that still helps the illusion of a watercolor wash, with tones broken by the brush, a decomposition not only produced by the air, by the day, by the sun, but a deliberate decomposition. This is the conviction of the skilled color printer, Mr. Gillot, a decomposition prepared in advance[50] by substances mixed with colors, by grass juices, by trade secrets that we do not know, and which make roses so pale, greens so deliciously yellow of old moss, blues so languidly sick,

---

[49] It is known that in the pulp of paper made with the bark of the shrub, called in Japanese *Kozo, Broussonetia papifera,* is added a milky substance, prepared with rice flower, and a gummy decoction of Hydrangea *paniculata* and *the* root of *Hibiscus Menichot.*

[50] Bracquemond told me that he had done similar tests on porcelain stains.

mauves where there is pigeon throat: a decomposition that, in the flat areas, where *color plays a role*, leads to veins, marbling, as found in malachites, turquoises, hard stones, and prepares these lingerie so extraordinary, so adorably cloudy, almost changing, and no longer having, if I dare say so, the immobility of a flat hue, under the decoration, under the richness of a dress's embroidery.

In the search for overall harmony, the printer goes even further: When he pulls the trigger, he does, yes, he throws dirt on it, resembling the imprint that the colored plate could have taken in the friction of a black plate, still wet; but as these dirt are only spread on the ground, the woodwork, that they never touch the faces, the flesh of women, it is indisputable that these dirt are the work of the printer, on the painter's indication.

Now, as we know, the impressions, coming from underneath this *art print,* were not, as some say, impressions for the general public, they were intended for delicate amateurs, men of letters, formerly living in Japan in the intimacy of artists, women of daimios, and they remained luxurious images, until they became, in the early years of this century, vulgar merchandise, in the hands of publishers, eager to make money and addressing the taste of the lower class, and on bad paper with badly cut wood, replacing the discreet, amortized, harmonious colorations of old prints, by screaming colorations, scoundrels: against the brutality of which, in 1830, the painter Hiroshige struggled in vain to bring back the eighteenth century colorations.

CATALOGUE RAISONNÉ

OF THE WORK

PAINTED AND ENGRAVED

OF THE

JAPANESE MASTER

MASTER'S PAINTINGS

Kakemonos. - Fans. - Drawings for
engraving. - Erotic Makimonos.

Japanese painting executed only in watercolor hardly occurs in three forms: kakemono or makimono; fan; sketch or rather finished drawing, the drawing has the appearance of an engraver's drawing, made by the master for the size of the woodcut; - and yet this drawing is still in Indian ink, the painter only trying his colors on a few black prints for him and his friends.

In the trips to Japan and the descriptions of the country's art objects, there is no mention of Outamaro kakemonos kept in museums or princes' collections, and Hayashi could only inform me about one that he has there.

It is a kakemono of a very delicate, very light, very clear water washing, representing, on brownish paper, in a medallion, three women's heads: the head of a Chinese princess wearing a metal bird; the head of a Japanese princess, her hair untied on her shoulders; the head of a court woman.

Mr. Anderson, in the large collection of *Japanese paintings,* formed by him, and transferred to the British Museum in 1882, does not mention any kakemonos from Outamaro, and Hayashi does not know any in America.

The kakemonos that we can describe are limited to these:

The kakemono of the woman who attaches a mosquito net over her child lying on the ground, belonging to Mr. Bing.

The kakemono of the Japanese woman unrolling a poetry, and the kakemono of the Japanese woman seen from behind, and with a hand that we do not see supporting the fallout of her belt and dress: two kakemonos that are my property.

Mr. Hayashi's kakemono, representing a dancer mimicking a dance of character, a quick sketch at first sight.

Finally, the three meters wide kakemono of Bing, to which it is perhaps necessary to give, for its counterpart, another kakemono of more or less the same size representing, splashed with gold, another "Green House" in the springtime, where more than forty women are painted, but where I do not find the character of Outamaro in its maturity, but which, at the very least, could be a kakemono from the artist's youth.

As for fans, Mr. Wakai, Mr. Hayashi's former partner, would have in Japan, on silver paper, an artistic fan of Outamaro, representing a full-length Japanese woman, of cursive work, but of great skill and charm, - a fan that would be mounted in kakemono.

For Outamaro's drawings made for engraving, we do not know any, as we know Hokusai's drawings among some amateurs, as we know Hokkeï's drawings among Mr. Duret

Outamaro also left makimonos, those rolls of several meters, where a composition unfolds in width, and where he would have put the best qualities of his talent.

Mr. Hayashi would possess in Japan one of these erotic scrolls, thirty-five centimeters high and five meters wide, barely tinted on Chinese ecru paper, and resembling some of Shunman's impressions: grayscales in a slightly purple hue, with little discreet coloring here and there, and comprising nine scenes of admirable execution. The owner declares that the expressions, attitudes, movements are so much of nature and life, that we forget that we are facing an erotic representation, and speaking of the finish and variety of the ornamentation of dresses, and in the middle of that, the value of the black lacquer of hair untied of women, he says that in his opinion, it is the most beautiful work known of Outamaro.

YELLOW BOOKS

(Kibiôshi)

From these little books, printed in black (17 centimeters high by 12 centimeters wide), here is a bibliography given to me by Hayashi:

BRIEF HISTORY OF A COQUETTISH GENTLEMAN. *Minari daïsûjin Riaku-yenghi.*

A small book, in 3 volumes, published in 1781.

ACCOUNT BOOK OF RECEIPTS FOR LIES. *Gantori-chô.*
A small book, in 3 volumes, published in 1783.

HISTORY OF SINCE[51]. *Sorekara Iraqi.*
Small volume published in 1784.

THE UNIVERSE THROUGH THE HEDGE. *Daïsensékai Kakinosoto.* Text by Sanva.

Small book, in 2 volumes, published in 1784.

DETAILS ON THE SECOND KAJIWARA LINK. *Kajiwara saiken Nidono-ô.* Text by Shibô Sanjin.

Small book, in 2 volumes, published in 1784.

---

[51] Many of the titles in these small volumes are almost untranslatable in French.

THE DEPTH OF THOUGHT THAT WE DON'T KNOW. *Hito-shirazu Omoïfukai.* Text by Shikibu.

Small book, in *2* volumes, published in 1784.

NITTA'S MILITARY CAPABILITY. *Nïtta tsusenki.* Text by Sadamarou.

Small book, in 2 volumes, published in 1784[52].

Outamaro would have let the years 1785, 1786, 1787 pass without publishing yellow books; he resumed publishing these little books in 1788.

THE YOSHIWARA'S SNOW WOMAN (on the [1st] day of the 8th month). *Yuki ouna Kuruwa hassaku.*

Small book without date.

THE SEVENTHS OF THE TWELVE ZODIACS. *Kammuri- Kotoba, Nanatsumé jûnihishiki.*

A small book, in 3 volumes, published in 1789.

STORIES ABOUT THE OPENING OF THE FURNACE. *Robiraki hanashi-Kutikiri.* These are tales on the occasion of the small celebration, which devotes, with each return of winter, the first use of heating for home and tea.

---

[52] Mr. Hayashi pointed out that the illustrations for these books had to be made before 1784, and that Outamaro's success had them printed all of a sudden. The following year, 1785, his two students, Mitimaro and Yukimaro, published four books, which proved, he said, that at that time Outamaro was no longer a young beginner.

Small book, in 2 volumes, published in 1789.

AOTO'S SAPÈQUE. *Tamamighaku Aoto-ghazéni.*
A small book, in 3 volumes, published in 1790.

HISTORY OF THE LONGEVITY OF YUTCHÔRÔ. *Yutchôrô Kotobuki banaski.*
A small book, in 3 volumes, published in 1790.

DUTIES TO THE TEACHER AND PARENTS ARE FUN. *Chûkô Asobishigoto.*
Small book, published in 1790.

INSTRUCTION ON THE SPOT BY THE EARS. *Sakusiki Mimigakumon.*
Small book, published in 1790.

TALES OF LOVE AFFAIRS I DON'T LIKE TO HEAR. *Ouwaki banashi.*
Small book, in 3 volumes, published in 1790[53].

Outamaro would have stopped, at that time, the publication of his little yellow books, enclosed, we see, between the year 1783 and the year 1790, where the history of the Aoto sapèque appeared.

---

[53] The handwritten book *Aohon Nempiô,* TABLE DES LIVRES JAUNES *avec les dates,* which Mr. Hayashi used to write this catalogue, does not mention the name Outamaro until 1781, where it begins, but it is very likely that Outamaro had to publish small yellow books before that date, under a pseudonym that is unknown.

To these yellow books, we must add the small books also printed in black, in mangwa format, which are:

THE BOUQUET OF SPEECH. *Yehon Koloba-nohana*, published in two volumes in 1787.

THE SPARROWS OF YEDO. *Yehon Yedo-suzume.*
Poems illustrated on the famous places of Yédo, published in three volumes in 1788.

POETRY, ON THE MILKY WAY. *Kiôka Yéhon Amamoghawa.* A beautiful volume with beautiful engravings, illustrated with twelve plates, and published by the famous publisher Tsutaya, in 1790.

SURUGHA'S DANCE. *Yehon Surugha-nomai.* Poems on the famous places of Yédo, published in three volumes, in 1790.

SCENES OF LIFE. *Yehon Tatoyébushi* (poems with rhythmic allusions), published in three volumes, undated.

Among these books printed in black, I still find in Mr. Bing's private collection a small book, entitled *Kannin boukouro,* SAC DE LA PATIENCE, with the epigraph: *Do not burst the cave of anger,* a small curious volume where the men have on their faces, human traits, replaced by characters, under which the Japanese represent good and bad geniuses, and where a board shows us a fisherman removing a quantity of these heads in his sparrowhawk.

Another small black book by Outamaro, part of the collection, entitled *Aké no harow,* NOUVEAU PRINTEMPS, was printed in 1802.

BOOKS IN COLOR[54]

THE SILVERY NATURE (snow). *Yehon Guin Sekai.*

The snow in Japan, in this country of mounds and picturesque trees, is a source of inspiration for poets.

And there, the admiration of the snow descends from the literate classes to the people. Hayashi quotes this word from a servant, fearing to stain the beautiful carpet of the ground, and shouting a clever one: "Ah ! the new snow ! this tea grounds, where will I throw it?"

This loving poetry about the exiled lover, from the charming words of this other servant: "Oh, please, madam, this morning, don't send me to the market, the little dog has bloomed the yard with his paws. I wouldn't want to erase that delicate painting with my big country hooves! »

This book, following a poetry competition, open at certain times of each year, and where these poems are published in one volume, was illustrated by Outamaro, with six color prints on the same theme as the one proposed to the poets: The snow.

THE MOON'S CRAZY ADMIRATION. *Yehon Kiô- qkétsubô.*
Inquarto book, illustrated with five double plates, published in 1789.

JAPANESE POEMS ON THE SPRING WALK. *Yehon Waka Yebisu.*
Inquarto book, illustrated with five double plates, published without date.

---

[54] I classify in this series the albums big or small, which have a text, a foreword, a preface.

THE CLOUD OF CHERRY BLOSSOMS. *Yehon Hanano-Kumo.*
In quarto book, published without date.

FLOWERS OF THE FOUR SEASONS. *Yehon Shiki-nohana.*
Compositions representing women, with flowers on the first and last
page of the volumes: yellow flowers of *Kirià japonica* for winter,
narcissus for spring, iris for summer, chrysanthemums for autumn.

In this volume, a charming impression represents an interior during
a storm, where we see a man closing the wooden shutters, a child crying,
a woman in the green half-light of a mosquito net blocking her ears for
fear of it: an impression from which Outamaro has taken up certain
details for his large board of THE STORM.

Book in two volumes, published in 1801.

FUGHEN FIGURE. *Fughenzô* (in Sanskrit *Samanta Chadra*),
Buddhist goddess of the Bodhisatawa class. Fughen is translated into a
universal sage.

This goddess is worshipped in Japan along with Manju, *Manjushiri-
satawa,* and in her illustration of this book, Outamaro refers to the
virtuous beauty of women.

An in-quarto book, illustrated with five double plates, published in
1770.

Of this goddess Fughen, represented on an elephant, Mr. Gonse has
a small color image, which he believes is part of an unknown book.

DIRECTORY OF GREEN HOUSES. *Seirô-Ychon Nenjû Ghiô-ji.*
Book printed with the collaboration of Kikumaro, Hidemaro,
Takimaro with a text by Jipensha Ikkou, and published by the publisher
Kazousaya Tûsouké, in the year 1804.

A small book, composed of the combination of ten images of

women in half-body.

A little book made up of the collection of ten images of women in bust, shown in every detail of their toilets-

A small book bearing the stamp of Wakai, where the daily occupations of women's lives in Japan are depicted, and in groups of two women, or a woman with a child.

This book and the other two, all three parts of Mr. Gillot's bibliographic rarities, seem to be of the good impression and circulation of the beginning of the century.

Finally, a small book from Mr. Duret's collection, entitled: *Women's Vice by Condition*, and Representative:

1° An old dancer; - 2° A koto mistress; - 3° a poetess; - 4° a courtesan; - 5° a nanny; - 6° a schinzô (courtesan apprentice); -7° a messenger of a princess; - 8° a widow; - 9° a dressing table; - 10° A doctor; - 11° An archer and bowmaker; - 12° A peasant woman; - 13° A log merchant; - 14° A sacred dancer, *niko;* - 1 5° A merchant; - 16° A *shiokumi* (the one who collects sea water for salt).

A charming example of a small volume of the great drawing of Outamaro and its sober coloring.

In the series of color books specially belonging to natural history, we know:

REMEMBRANCE OF THE LOW TIDE. *Shiohi-no-tsuto*:

Poems on shells by members of a Literary Society and the last board representing the game of Kai-awassé, six double shell plates.

Book published around 1870.

THE INSECTS CHOSEN. *Yehon Mushi-yérabi:*

Books with several editions, the last ones being quite inferior to the first ones, and the most complete editions containing 15 plates.

Book published in 1788, with a preface by Toriyama Sékiyen in mind.

THE HUNDRED POUNDERS (Bird Poetry Contest). *Yehon Momotidori,* book published by Tsutaya Juzabrô.

Mr. Gonse has two editions of this book.

The first edition contains eight double-sheet compositions.

The second edition, in two volumes, contains fifteen compositions, in the following order:

First volume.

1. Owl sleeping on an old tree trunk, near several robins. - — 2. Water chickens and cranes. - — 3. Warbler and sparrow, on a flowery branch of white chrysanthemum. - — 4. Pigeons, in the middle of *mummy hi* leaves and pine needles, littering the ground. - — 5. Nice and jay, on a dead plum tree branch. - — 6. Kingfisher on a reed stem, and mandarin ducks. - — 7. Eagle and stipple, on a branch of flowering plum tree.

Second volume.

8. Tit on a branch of a flowering peach tree. - — 9. Quails and broom rail, in the middle of the rushes. - — 10. Big beak and woodpecker, on a pine trunk. —11. Ordinary pheasant, pheasant hen and wagtail, in the middle of the rocks. - — 12. Chinese pheasant, and flying swallow. - — 13. Chloris, on bamboo twigs. - — 14. Regulus on a branch of flowered broom, and herons in the reeds. - — 15. Rooster and hen.

SUITE OF THE HUNDRED CRIERS. *Yehon Momotidori Kohen.*

Isn't that the second volume, considered as the second edition of *Yehon Momotidori?*

A book to be attached to the HUNDRED SELLERS, is this book that only Mr. Gonse owns in Paris, and of which we are not sure, that the number of ten plates is the number of plates of the complete book. It is entitled: COPIES OF FOREIGN BIRDS *by a Nagasaki official for presentation to the shogun.*

1. Long-tailed parakeet. - — 2. Sansonnet, in the branches of a cherry tree in bloom. - — 3. Lark, in the middle of the peonies. - — 4. Hochequeue, among flowers of water. - — 5. Silver pheasants from China, rooster and hen. - — 6. European grey partridge. - — 7. Oriole pecking at Japanese medlars. - — 8. Robin, on a branch of momichi. - — 9. Jay, on a branch of flowering camellia. - — 10. Gelinotte.

In addition to these series, there would be a series of large birds in a format larger than the "Hundred Screamers", of which Mr. Gonse has an impression representing a falcon on a branch of a plum tree in bloom, and of which Mr. Bing has a large stork, very straight, standing on a branch of a fir tree, next to a nest where there are seven young, crying out in alarm, in front of an unknown danger.

To these books on shells, insects, birds, let's join these fragments of books related to botany.

Mr. Gillot owns the separate plates of a book, which is probably one of the many books made there, for the composition of bouquets and their arrangement in vases: a talent for pleasure that is, in Japan, part of the education of a distinguished young girl.

There are seven of these black plates with a few avaricious yellow colors. They are all signed by Outamaro.

Four other larger plates of a precious impression, coming from Japan in a batch of Outamaro, and which are attributed to him, but of a drawing and a slightly Chinese coloring, seem to me to be of a dubious attribution.

Among the decorative plates, borrowed by Outamaro from natural history, let us also mention plates from Mr. Bing's private collection, of great style, in a somewhat archaic tonality.

These are two impressions: one, where two crabs drag beside a sea plant, the other, where a chrysanthemum stem can be seen, with a foot surrounded by a bale of rice straw, leaning on a Japanese spade.

And two more plates of a series of which we should only have isolated impressions in France, and of which the second was printed on ordinary paper and crepe. The first represents two boxes of flowers superimposed above a Japanese well; the second represents a toad holding in its mouth a vase in the shape of a half-unrolled lotus leaf, in which is a stem of a shrub with yellow and violet flowers.

Finally, during the printing of the proofs, I found two plates of this series; one is a turtle carrying, in a vase similar to that of the toad, a bunch of chrysanthemums; the other is a Yebisu god, holding above his two hands, in a vase of sparterie (hard vegetal fiber), a branch of cherry tree in flower.

Let us now give the few isolated color plates published by Outamaro in the works illustrated by these colleagues.

In *Otoko-foumi-outa*, a COLLECTION OF LIGHT POEMS illustrated by several artists, and containing such a beautiful plate of Hokousai, Outamaro drew the inside of a tea house, where in a room decorated with a screen, representing the Fuzi-yama, a snack is prepared, among women, including one carrying a bird in a cage.

In *Haru-no-iro*, COULEUR DU PRINTEMPS, a book by *Kioka* (light poems) illustrated by various artists, published in 1794, Outamaro drew a leaf representing a mirror ironer.

In *Haigu-rakou-rhitou-tsou*, PORTRAITS OF THE ACTORS (OF YÉDO by Toyokouni and his pupil Kounimasa (1789-1793), Outamaro, in addition to the frontispiece, composed with the accessories of Nô's dance, drew the small board representing a sitting actor, who smokes, looking at the exit of three women from the theatre.

LARGE PRINTINGS

(*Nishiki-Yé.*)

These large impressions, generally composed of three, five, and even seven boards, in this country of folding screens and sliding doors, are glued together at the ends of each other, without a glass that defends the charming coverings of these movable walls[55] from air damage. Sometimes the compositions of famous masters are mounted in a cloth border, enclosed in a lacquer rod.

PRINTS COMPOSED OF ONE OR TWO PLATES

THE THREE WAYS.

Board that represents three faces of women, the way of laughing, the way of crying, the way of getting angry. These women, I think, a little grey sake, are offered as a translation of the Japanese proverb that says: "*When you have drunk, the way comes out*".

A single board, which can be either that of a non-continued series or a separate board.

Composition where we see a woman crouching on her heels, making a monkey dance on the top of a screen, which two children are watching. Red characters, sown on the board, teach us that a superstition of the country wants this dance to drive smallpox out of

---

[55] Cola explains the tired, smoky state of most of these impressions, and the difficulty of meeting them in the conditions where European prints are available.

houses.

Hayashi believes that the composition is complete in a single plate.

Pair of courtesans.

Prints composed of two plates.

TRIPTYCHAL IMPRESSIONS

THE FIRST DAY OF THE YEAR.

Triptych impression described above.

Women mounted on an improvised platform, tying up pine branches, colocynth, pieces of poetry in the air.

Preparations for a New Year's Day celebration.

Triptych impression.

THE WEDDING.

Triptych impression described above.

The wedding after the ceremony.

The bride changes her costume, in front of a large lacquer mirror, lying on the ground, among women preparing her new toilet.

Triptych impression.

Seven women from the courtyard of a daimio, seven long and elegant women, topped with this cornet made of a silk band rolled around their hairstyle, stopped in a landscape where a curtain of iridescent greens, flowered in all colors, rose to their waist, masking the whole bottom of their dresses.

Compositions of the noblest style and rarest rarity.

Triptych impression.

In a landscape, all pinky of the cherry blossom, under a purple hanging, is gathered a large society of noble women. In the background, we see a rich norimon lying on the ground; in the foreground on the right, a servant has custody of a sake barrel.

Triptych impression.

EMBARKING A PRINCESS FOR A RIVER CROSSING.

With the large trunks with dresses already lowered into the boat, the princess embarked, escorted by a woman carrying the smoking room, a woman in charge of the perfume bag and the small ceremonial sword.

Triptych impression.

Princess descending, on a step board, from a large trolley with lacquered wheels, silk linings, an imperial trolley, while a woman presents her with a fan, and she is looked at by two women, one of whom is lying on a terrace, and again by the prince, hardly visible behind a blind.

Triptych impression.

DANCING A GUESHA IN A DAIMIO PALACE.

Triptych impression described above.

Visit of a woman of the nobility to another woman of the nobility.

The two women walk towards each other, at the threshold of a house, in a small garden, where a large chrysanthemum bush rises in the middle.

Triptych impression.

REST ON A TERRACE ON THE BANKS OF THE SOUMIDA.

A young prince, in a society of women, one of whom wears her dress from above, where you can see through the light black cloth, a sealed letter, perhaps intended for the woman taking the garment with her.

Triptych impression.

A princess comes out of her norimon to take a cool break by the sea, while one of her wives puts slippers under her feet, and another opens a parasol on her head.

Triptych impression.

A daimio on horseback, a falcon on his fist, crosses a small stream, in the escort of women, one carrying his spear, another his sword, and one last a falcon. The Fuzi-yama in the distance.

Triptych impression.

Inside a daimio where a women's society amuses itself by watching a young prince dance in a black dress, purple skirt trousers, with his fan lowered on his hip.

Triptych impression.

A flat boat slid over the water by a man weighing on a long bamboo. In the middle, a daimio, a falcon on his fist, and surrounded by women, one of whom turns around to kiss her child on her back.

Triptych impression.

Japanese women escorting an imperial chariot. In front, a princess walks on whose head a woman from her suite holds a rich parasol open, and we notice, in the escort, another woman carrying on her back a quiver full of arrows.

Triptych impression.

Two women walking a small daimio carrying on their fist, in place of the future falcon, a sparrow; one of the women holds under her arm the child's little sword. In the board on the right, a merchant, carrying two baskets on her shoulder at the end of a stick, offers an eggplant to a walker.

Triptych impression.

A princess descended from her imperial chariot, holding a strip of paper covered with poetry to a young man, kneeling a few steps away from her. This poetry would be a declaration of love, and in his shyness, the young man has like a fainting of love, whose failure is supported by a wife of the princess, leaning over the teenager.

Triptych impression.

NOBLE DANCE.

Schizuka, Yoritomo's mistress, to the sound of tambourines and flutes of musicians mimicking a dance of character, the red fan of her dress, lowered with one hand, an arm waving the floating of a scarf over her head.

The curious thing about its composition so that it is not too historical is that Yoritomo, the illustrious lover of women, is represented by a woman who is supposed to represent him.

Triptych impression.

Three groups of one man and one woman, seen up to the waist.

Composition allusive to the journey of Narihira, great lord poet, travelling east of Kioto, to go to Fuzi-yama, in a time when the city of Yédo did not exist.

Triptych impression.

In the middle of tall wild grasses, women walking with lanterns on, and looking for a man that a woman is trying to hide behind her.

An episode of the novel where Aghémaki hides Soukéroku.

SPRING FESTIVAL WHERE WE GO TO LOOK IN THE PINE
SHOOT CAMPAIGN.

In this board, among women loaded with branches of green trees,
we see two girls arguing, tearing a large pine branch out of their hands.

Triptych impression.

ADMIRING WALK OF THE CHERRY BLOSSOMS IN THE
COUNTRYSIDE.

A board of the beginnings of Outamaro, where he is not yet him,
where he has not yet found the slenderness of his women's height, and
their long oval.

Triptych impression.

On the banks of a torrent, a house, from which a women's society
descends to watch the current full of cherry blossoms. Among the
women left in the house is a tall girl, holding a doll in her arms.

Triptych impression.

A society of women looking down from a terrace, at the time of the
flowering of peonies, a river that seems to flow from these flowers, so
much the ripple carry them away.

Triptych impression.

MUSIC, GAMES, PAINTING, WRITING, THE FOUR PLEASANT
OCCUPATIONS.

A society of women, sitting on their heels on the ground, in childish
admiration for kakemonos spread out on the sand of a small garden;
while, in one pavilion, a woman writes a letter next to a woman making
music and, in another pavilion very far away, two Japanese are playing.

Triptych impression.

PRIVACY CONCERNS.

In the midst of women working on their own sex, a young Japanese man playing in a corner of an apartment with a girl in a *sougorokou* - a game that looks exactly like our backgammon game.

Triptych impression.

TRAPPING DANCE.

Two women kneeling, trying to remove a cup from the middle of a large loose knot of a silk cord they are twisting, lying on the ground. The loser is condemned to dance until she has been able to grasp the cup dexterously, in the middle of the fast spinning of the rope, which takes her wrist, if she misses it.

Triptych impression.

A beach covered with people, by the sea, where boats full of people pass by. In a corner, an angler, attention to the fish that bites, while smoking his pipe. In the middle of the board, a child having fun dancing a crab at the end of his line.

Triptych impression.

A river where, on two boats, men and women fish by angling, and where, in the air, you see a grey fish wriggling on a hook.

Triptych impression.

Walk in the surroundings of Kamakouro, where you can see a woman in a *kago* placed on land (the kago is the bourgeois norimon).

Triptych impression.

Japanese women in the countryside, one of whom holds her child tenderly against her chest, while a little Japanese boy raises his hands in the air, in the amazement of a flight of birds flying through the sky.

Triptych impression.

THE HARVEST OF THE KHAKIS.

Women falling big trees with a hooked bamboo, these orange species.

Triptych impression,

THE GREAT BRIDGE OF SOUMIDA.

Nine women, one of whom holds a child playing in her arms, nine elegant women, standing or leaning on the bridge crossing, talking, venting, watching the water of the river flow.

Triptych impression.

Walk of women and children on the banks of the Soumida.

A representation of the night, of its dense, deep, mysterious darkness, which Japanese masters like to reproduce: a composition giving you the spectacle of the illumination carried out by women's summer dresses, on this beach in the black of a lacquer plate, in front of this dark water that crosses a bridge with endless pilings, a bridge that has the character of a projection of a magic lantern, under a sky of a dark blue, glittering stars so numerous, that they seem snowflakes.

Triptych impression.

Pilgrimage of women, barefoot, in the flow of the sea, on the beach of Isé.

Triptych impression described above.

An open gallery overlooking the gardens, a gallery populated by women, one of whom dresses a child, and where, from the outside, a servant holds out to a woman, on the doorstep, a basin and a red cotton towel, for the child's washing-up.

Triptych impression.

FIREFLIES.

Triptych impression described above.

A beach, by the sea, in the middle of which stands a green islet, a beach where women walk, one of whom leans on a high bamboo. On the right a man attaches his shoe, on the left in a kago lying on the ground, a woman smokes next to a woman sitting near the small vehicle and lights her pipette.

Triptych impression.

A journey on the water, during which the boat is docked by a boat, where the fisherman's wife offers fish to the travelers in the cabin, on the roof of which fans a large fan, the boatman who lies on it.

Triptych impression.

A woman angling in a large boat, driven by a boatwoman, and who is accosted by a boat, where a fisherman is casting her net.

Triptych impression.

A boat, in which a naked girl ties a cloth around her hair, ready to jump from the boat into the water, where other children are already swimming.

Triptych impression.

PORTRAITS OF THE CURRENT FAMOUS BEAUTIFUL WOMEN
(Honest Women).

Composition printed on a yellow background.

Triptych impression.

THE CHILDREN'S CLASS.

Composition inspired by the play entitled: *Tenarai-Kagami.*

Triptych impression.

THREE WAYS TO GET CHILDREN TO READ.

Triptych impression[56].

---

[56] On the education of children, let us give this curious note by Mr. Hayashi in the publication on Japan, published in the *Paris illustrated book.*

The education, at the time of publication of these prints, was given by the parents and was called: *Education of the Family Garden.*

It consisted: 1° in learning to read the Japanese alphabet and the most useful Chinese characters; 2° in the area to enter into the child's idea the moral principles of Confucius, summarized as duties towards teachers, parents, friends.

It was customary for parents to tell children in the evening, after dinner, all kinds of national legends or stories of China that could serve as a model of conduct.

When a child was not wise, he was threatened by being told that he would not hear this or that story, and he obeyed immediately. Thus, before reaching the age where we learn to read, children knew many things about life. Because they were not told Bluebeard tales, Buddhist miracles, they were told the biographies of famous men.

There were also private institutions, run by teachers, who not only taught

CHILDREN PLAYING WAR.

A little boy on the battlefield, another carrying the flag, another waving the general sign: an assembly at the end of the shaft of a spear, small water bottles falling down around a large water bottle, fixed straight.

Impression that I have reason to believe a triptych impression.

THE CULTURE OF ENGRAVINGS IN YÉDO, THE FAMOUS PRODUCTION OF THIS CITY

Triptych impression already described.

An isolated impression, which fell before my eyes, would make me believe that Outamaro drew another composition of three plates on the same subject.

This impression represents the wall of a shop covered in colorful images, in the middle of which are hung three kakemonos, while a kneeling Japanese defiles a packet of impressions, while a woman sits on a platform between two or three painted sheets, a cone, a brush for a moment abandoned, arranges a pin of her hair, while a child on her knees hands her a sheet of paper, still white.

---

children to read and write, but also taught them politeness and propriety. These institutions were named *Tera, a* Buddhist temple, and the students were called *Terako,* "children of Tera", the education having been given initially by Buddhist priests.

THE WOMEN IN THE KITCHEN.

In the two rare printed sheets, which we know so far from the composition, one woman blows fire into a bamboo, another takes a teapot from a stove, whose water spreading has made a cloud of steam, and one last peels an eggplant.

The third sheet that Hayashi never met is nowhere to be found.

Triptych impression.

Woman near a stove surrounded by vials and bottles, blowing glass into a bamboo, and to which another woman brings a box filled with small sticks.

Impression that I believe triptych.

Production of white sake, lady's sake, a soft, barely fermented sake.

A press, in which the fermentation of the rice gushes out under the stone wheel, pressed by the huge wooden arm, which two women, weighing on it, turn like riding horses.

The representation of an industrial factory, a little ideal, a manufacture taking place in a palace, and where the two women, doing the job of riding horses, look like Allegories dressed in the most beautiful dresses of the Sunrise Empire.

Triptych impression.

THE DRY CLEANERS.

A large strip of purple cloth, stretched between two trees, drying in the sun, which a dyer cleans, and which a walker grabs as she passes, and on which, held by her mother, a child who wants to kiss her sister through the cloth, who makes her face look purple, leans.

Triptych impression.

THE DIVERS.

The three edible shell fisherwomen, called in Japan *awabi*.
Triptych impression described above.

THE DIVERS.

Composition different from the first.
Triptych board described above.

SALTWATER CARRIERS *(Shiokumi).*

They are represented in their picturesque arrangement, with the curved stick supporting the two buckets, and their reed petticoats, resembling large loincloths. On the other side of the water, in the distance, the roofs of salt works where they will carry sea water.

Triptych impression.

POETRY SNACK.

One of the plates represents a woman, drawing a poem with a brush. The title of the composition is written on a large makimono at the top of the board.

Triptych impression.

An interior, where a half-lying woman is leaning on one hand, lying on the ground, and there now lifted in a graceful movement.

Plate where a large piece of poetry is printed in a red frame in width.

Board that I suppose a triptych impression.

THREE WOMEN COMPARED TO THREE PHILOSOPHERS.

Triptych impression.

THREE POETS (represented by women).
Triptych impression.

THE SNOW, THE MOON, THE FLOWER.
In a compartment, a woman, who still has the brush in her hand with which she has just written a poem. Near her a friend, her hands turned over, twisted in a stretch of grace of her outstretched arms, along her side. In another compartment, a woman reading a letter that a servant brings to her.
Triptych impression.

SAKE, which can be translated as something like this, THOSE WHO HAVE DRUNK TOO MUCH, *seven different postures* (drunkenness).
It is the representation, under a woman leaning on the cylinder surrounded by sparterie, of the Morose Drunkenness, the Chatty Drunkenness, the Dancing Drunkenness, the Hallucinated Drunkenness who makes music with a fan on a broom - and even the Dirty Drunkenness, figured by taking the nipples of a big woman disheveled by an old skeleton men, in a third very rare board, and which brings the number of drunkenness to eight instead of seven.
Triptych impression.

Women bringing sake barrels, around another woman, dancing a fan in their hands, and below which red-haired beings, *shôjô,* sake geniuses, lap up, crouching on the ground, like animals, huge cups of Japanese alcohol.
Triptych impression.

A celebration, on a terrace overlooking a gulf, with the most rugged banks, in which, near a snack served, a woman and a man play a Japanese game, where one counts on the fingers of both hands, opposite each other.

A composition that is very imaginative in Chinese taste, and where the coloring, held almost absolutely in the three shades, yellow, green, purple, is the coloring of the porcelains of the green family.

Triptych impression.

Yoritomo's cranes.

Printing already described.

In a mountainous landscape, women carrying small bamboo cupboards, on their shoulders, one of them with a washer, by a stream.

A composition that recalls, under the veil of allegory, the death of the terrible Shutendôji brick from Oyeyama Mountain, killed by Kintoki and his heroic friends, dressed as priests. However, these women wear on their backs wardrobe boots, in which priests, Shutendôji's vigilantes, wore Buddha and other religious figures.

Triptych impression.

The exiled prince between the two salt carriers, Matzugazé and Mourasamé.

Triptych impression already described.

THE THREE CUPS.

Allegorical composition between sennins, men and women of longevity.

Triptych impression.

SPRING OCCUPATIONS.

Allusive piece to the seven gods of Japanese Olympus.

The Japanese Olympus is composed of Benten, Bishamon, Daikoku, Yébisu, Fukuroku-Jiu, Hoteï, Juro, the seven *Kamis* : Benten, the goddess of arts and manual dexterity, represented by the head girded with a golden crown, and usually playing the *biwa, the* four-string mandolin; - Bishamon, the god and patron saint of soldiers, battleship and helmeted, and usually holding, in his left hand, a small pagoda, where are enclosed the souls of the devotees, whom he has the mission to defend; - Yébisu, the father of Japan's food industry, with the hundreds of fish, crabs, mollusks, edible seafood from its seas, and its twenty-six species of mussels and shellfish, the god of the sea, the patron saint of fishermen, recognizable by his big butt in checkered pants, his broad laugh of osque polichinella, his line with a *tay, the* Japanese's favorite fish; - Daikoku, the god of wealth, with a mallet in his hand, sitting on a bag of rice; - Fukuroku-Jiu, the god of longevity, an old man with a white beard, a conical forehead and disproportionately high by his continuous meditation, leaning on a travel stick; - Hoteï, the god of childhood, carrying on his back a barrel, filled with sweets for the children who are wise, and who is sometimes depicted with eyes all around his head, in order to see the evil children; - finally Juro, god of prosperity, most often mounted on a stag, and depicted under a square cap, unrolling a large scroll, an edict of general happiness.

Triptych impression.

AUTHENTIC DAIKOKU BRUSH.

A board depicts Daikoku, in front of a small table, doing his portrait on a kakemono, surrounded by women, one of whom, kneeling, rolls a portrait already made of the god, while he is dominated by another elegant and charming woman, who is about to hand him a sheet of paper so that the portrait he is doing, once finished, he will do another for her.

Triptych impression.

GOOD HARVEST YEAR.

Satirical composition about the gods having fun performing a play.

Triptych impression.

THE WEDDING OF THE GODDESS BENTEN.

A caricatured composition depicting the goddess' marriage, with a figure with a big head, in the middle of six grotesque models, depicting the six gods - this in the laughter of women - a laugh that makes the face of a *mousmé* a figure similar to the figures, libidinous and comic, of some small ivory masks.

Triptych impression.

THE GODS OF JAPANESE OLYMPUS.

Another untitled composition, where we see, to the right of the board, a little girl palpating the enormous cardboard belly of a figuration of Yébisu, while a young woman presents him with a bottle of sake in brown pottery, where his portrait is shaped; on the other side a Fuyoroku-Jiu, whose gigantic forehead is made by an amphora topped by a teapot: a Fukoroku-Jiu scaffolded by children, while in the middle the goddess Benten plays the schamisen.

Triptych impression.

A meeting of women in a large pleasure boat.

Allegorical composition, or by various symbols, in this boat whose bow is made of a gigantic carved and colored Ho-ô, the seven women who appear there represent the seven gods and goddesses of Olympus: Hoteï, Juro, Bishamon, Daikoku, Yébisu, Fukuroku-Jiu, Benten.

Triptych impression.

A decorative boat at the bow finished by a dragon, and populated by women representing Olympus, by the port they make on them of an attribute of a god from there: one holding in hand the hammer of Daikoku, the other the turtle of Jiurô, finally another holding at the end of a long bamboo passed over his shoulder, a screen and a box to dispatch, the attribute of another god.

Composition different from the previous one.

Triptych impression.

A boat with a hull finishing at the top of the Ho-ô, and containing a Japanese Olympus, represented by children depicting Daikoku, Bischamon, etc., and the boat mounted on wheels is dragged by women, one of whom, crouched on her side, is nursing an infant, playing a Hoteï at the breast.

This impression, based on the model of a large children's toy, is curious by its date: *New Year's Day 1805.* Outamaro died in 1806.

Triptych impression.

THE PLEASURES OF TAIKÔ WITH ITS FIVE WOMEN IN THE EAST OF THE CAPITAL

Board described above.

THE MODERN MUSICIANS.

One of the musicians holding the ivory plectrum in her hand, which she will play.

Triptych impression.

THE MODERN GIRLS OF THE FUTURE.

Triptych impression.

THE ANTECHAMBER OF A TEA HOUSE, during Niwaka (the carnival).

In front of a courtesan and a Japanese seated at the back of the room, stand on the right the *guesha,* dressed as young boys, their hair cut, while a *taikomati* crouched on the ground, and making the gesture of wiping his forehead, chats for a moment with the courtesan, having placed beside him his disguise, trumpet and Korean hat, a pointed green hat, topped with feathers.

Triptych impression.

COURTESANS GATHERED IN THE VIP LOUNGE.

In the first proofs, the background is white, in the reprints, the background is filled, on the three plates, by the great Hô-ô, which we see painted by Outamaro, in the last plate of the second volume of the Green Houses.

Triptych impression.

GREAT CELEBRATION OF THE FIRST EVENING.

Two courtesans in a corridor, looking into the living room, where the party is taking place; a woman squatting in a room next door, looking like she is listening to music.

Triptych impression.

IN THE MORNING IN A GREEN HOUSE.

The farewell of a woman to a Japanese man, whose head and chest can be seen as he descends the stairs. In the middle board a woman talking with a friend, her hand resting on the kidneys of a service man, squatting from behind next to her. In the right board, a woman in conversation, through a mosquito net, with a Japanese man smoking his pipe: a conversation that a long and elegant woman listens to, half masked by a screen.

Triptych impression.

Flower boat filled with women sitting in the cabin, surmounted on the roof of the smoking boatman, a bare thigh and leg, shamelessly thrown over the railing.

Triptych board.

Two courtesans in bust, each holding, on a lacquered tray, a doll representing famous wrestlers of the time, each of whom bears his name on his petticoat: one named Hiraïshi, the other Raïdu,

Triptych impression or maybe a series of three for album.

THE THEATRE DISGUISED IN GREEN HOUSES.

In the garden of a Green House, a woman brings on a tray of black lacquer, for the amusement of courtesans, a large doll holding an open parasol, which is a bit of a caricature of a well-known actor.

Triptych impression.

Women of a Green House occupied with an illumination: some putting lights in red lanterns, others hanging them from a vine arbor, filled with wisteria in Hours.

Triptych impression.

A SUMMER EVENING.

Near a bridge lit by lanterns, the river, all covered with boats, filled with women, one of whom is leaning over the water, is washing a red lacquer sake bowl.

Triptych board.

PRINTS COMPOSED OF FIVE PLATES

THE NEW YEAR'S EVE MARKET.

Printing composed of five plates, described above.

BOYS' DAY.

Printing composed of five plates, described above.

THE STREET OF YÉDO SOUROUGA-TCHÔ, IN FRONT OF THE SILK SHOPS.

Shops closed by curtains, and under the rise of which we see, in the background, the watch of fabrics spread out in front of the buyers, sitting in a circle on the ground.

Printing of five plates.

THE FLOWERS OF THE FIVE FESTIVALS.

Five women, under a purple mantling, sown with cherry blossoms, having near them in a vase or wall lamp, a flowering shrub of the season, where the celebration takes place.

Printing composed of five plates.

Walk of noble women and children, under blue parasols. Following them walks a servant carrying a canteen in a bag, and the sake barrel.

Printing composed of five plates.

THE SHOWER.

Printing composed of five plates, described above.

SINGERS, FLOWERS OF YEDO.

Printing composed, I believe, of five plates.

THE MUSICIANS:

A series of five women, squatting on a purple mat, and playing *schamisen, biva, koma-fouyè, koto, tossoumi.*

Charming compositions topped by a decorative band of delicious taste: a pink band with white cherry blossoms.

Printing composed of five plates.

In the street, women, children, and in the middle, on the back of the porters, the trunks for clothes, the trunks containing deliveries made by the stores.

Printing composed, I believe, of five plates.

OPENING EVENING OF THE SOUMIDA.

A sky, where a fireworks display explodes in a night full of stars, and on the water, a crowd of women's boats, in the middle of boatmen's disputes.

Printing composed of five plates.

Japanese women on a terrace, on the banks of a river, whose other bank contains, in its green landscape, a large bridge on piles. Lying, squatting, kneeling, these women read, drink tea, make music.

Printing composed of five plates.

PROCESSION OF CHILDREN.

A playful children's march, one of whom carries an iron spear, topped with a feathered tassel.

Printing probably composed of five plates.

THE BIG CLEANING OF A GREENHOUSE AT THE END OF THE YEAR.

Printing composed of five plates, already described.

PRINTS COMPOSED OF SIX PLATES

THE SIX TAMAGAWA.

Women's walk in the countryside, where a child walks in a stream, near a washing machine beating clothes with a roller.

PRINTS COMPOSED OF SEVEN PLATES

Procession of the Korean ambassador reproduced in a *Niwaka* by gueshas.

Printing composed of seven plates, described above.

PRINTED KAKEMONOS

In a catalogue of the Outamaro Color Printed Work, one cannot ignore these narrow strips of height, generally measuring 25 centimeters by 60 centimeters: these printed kakemonos, which are in Japan the art paintings of the people's homes, and which are surrounded by an economical paper frame, playing quite well both the arrangements and the designs and the brilliance of the silk fabrics, serving as a frame for the kakemonos by the masters' hands.

They are almost always pyramidal compositions, where a man and a woman overhanging themselves, amputated by the narrowness of the band, offer only pieces, slices of their bodies to the eye.

In the infinite number of these kakemonos, which are for the most part of a rather fast execution, and without variety in the motifs, and willingly repeating themselves with some insignificant changes, there are some of them neater, more successful, and which *doing so* approaches the good *neshiki-y*. I mention as samples some of them belonging to Mr. Gonse, Mr. Gillot, Mr. Hayashi.

Two women whose attention is drawn to something happening to their right; one of them holds against her the large umbrella hat she pulled from above her head.

Near a man holding and twisting a piece of cloth or paper in his hands, a woman covering her mouth with her sleeve up.

Woman standing in the night, dressed in a pigeon-throat dress sown with flowers, a half-open dress, which shows one of her breasts, above a woman sitting on her heels.

A woman walking in a gust of wind, holding with one hand the black hood of her head that flies away, pressing against her the swollen folds and lifted up from her wide dress.

An elegant Japanese woman in a purple dress, with two large Ho-oh wings spread out, and behind her, a lacquer tray mounted on a rich foot.

Woman holding against her a child who is reaching for a small mill, which is turned over her head by another woman.

A printed kakemono, quite superior, to the wrapped tones, to the *greasiest* tones, and a kakemono that I saw in Mr. Gillot's house, which represents a woman standing, leaning against a latticework, above a woman squatting, playing with an inverted screen.

Let's finish with four printed kakemonos, of offline quality, from Mr. Bing's private collection.

A kakemono showing a pretty guesha, wearing silver pins, leaning against the handle of a schamisen.

A kakemono representing a woman leaning towards a young girl, on whose back is a child, where the impression is similar to the impression of the most delicate color plates of Outamaro.

A kakemono where we see at the feet of a woman, a naked child, lying on the ground, who wrapped his head around the train's head in the woman's black gauze dress, so that his face appears tinged with the black weft and flowered with the flowers of the transparent fabric.

A very original kakemono. At the top, a woman with a fish on the end of her hook in the sky; at the bottom, a young man leaning out of the boat, and filling a cup, in the reflection of her bust in the water, - the most real reflection a painter has ever made.

ALBUMS

(Series of color prints.)

A HUNDRED FANTASTIC TALES.

One of the boards represents a room, where a Japanese hides his
head on the ground, under the sleeves of his robe, in front of the
appearance of two larvae: one with black skeleton parts piercing his
physical flesh; the other with his skull with huge empty orbits, in which
there are two small black spots, and drawing a bloody tongue, which
leaves the hole in his mouth, like a flame that the wind drives away.

Series whose number of impressions is not indicated by the word
cent, which, in Japanese, does not have the precise and fixed meaning
it has in French.

GOOD DREAMS *are all won.*

It is this series of dreams of the girl, the *prostitute, the old servant
of the samurai: dreams described above.*

Series of prints, the number of which is not indicated.

THE FOUR SLEEPERS.

Curious sequel, where the small vignette on the right, at the top of
the plate, making the mark of the series, is a large vignette imitating the
drawing of Indian ink, of an old master, that interprets, caricatures,
Outamaro in its color printing.

Thus, in the board I have before me, the vignette represents a
sleeping priest with two children lying at his feet, and behind him a

tiger, and the composition of Outamaro represents a woman sleeping with two children asleep at his feet, and a cat behind her.

Series composed of 3 plates.

THE FOUR POETIC ELEMENTS: *The Flower, the Bird*, the *Air, the Moon.*

Series of 4 prints.

SUMMER CLOCK.

Series of 12 prints.

FLOWERS OF THE WORD.

A series of prints, the number of which is not indicated, but which is very large.

THE SEVEN POETESSES.

A series of women, in yellow medallions, on white embossed leaves, of a very delicate execution.

Series of 7 prints.

FOUR POEMS BY FEMALE POETS.

Series of 4 prints.

Compositions, at the top of which the legend refers to the *Hundred Screamers*, and the fan, through which the legend passes, depicts a crab, a toad.

A series of imitations by men, in their attitude, their circumvention, their deformation, a series of very serious imitations of the crab, the toad, etc., etc., and this under women all disheveled, their breasts in the air.

Series of prints, the number of which is not indicated.

THE GREAT WARRIOR SAKATA-NO-KINTOKI AND HIS MOTHER YAMA-OUWA.

A series of boards show the terrible wild woman with uncultured black hair, with her mahogany-colored infant.

Several series.

THE TWELVE PAINTINGS OF THE SCENES OF THE FORTY-SEVEN RONINS, *formed by the most beautiful women.*

First suite.

Series of 12 prints.

THE FIVE FAMILY LIFE CELEBRATIONS.

In the old Japan, there were five major festivals. It was New Year's Day; - the third day of the third month; - the Feast of the Girls, - the fifth day of the fifth month; - the Feast of the Boys[57], - the seventh day of the seventh month; - the Feast of the Bride and Groom, - the ninth day of the ninth month; - the Feast of the Chrysanthemums, or the Feast of the Retirement of the Vulgar Life, to enter a philosophical or poetic life.

Series of 5 prints.

THE FLOWERS OF THE FIVE FESTIVALS.

---

[57] During the Boys' Day, each Japanese, who has had a boy in the year, climbs in front of his door at the top of a huge bamboo pole, a paper fish (*nohori*). The air, rushing into his mouth, swells the whole body, and we see it floating slightly in the wind. The figured fish is a carp, which rises from the torrents with a strong tailstroke; it symbolizes the energy, which we wish to the young man, to overcome the difficulties of life.

Series of five prints.

WOMEN'S ENTERTAINMENT AT THE FIVE FESTIVALS OF THE YEAR.

One of the plates depicts a woman looking at a huge lantern, where a man is very skilfully depicted, dressed as a cat, dancing to the music of a guesha.

Series of 5 prints.

FLOWERED CARDBOARD OF THE POEMS OF THE FIVE FESTIVALS.

The cardboard is the small vignette signing the series, and which, in each plate, instead of an image, contains a poem.

Series whose number is not indicated.

THE SEVENTH SIGN OF THE ZODIAC.

Series of prints, the number of which is not indicated.

THE LANTERN FESTIVAL.

Suite of a smaller format than the other printing suites.

This feast of lanterns takes place on the 13th, 14th, 15th of the seventh month; it is, in vulgar style, "the cracked back of ghosts", *Tamamatsouri,* and corresponds to our All Saints.

In the main room of each house, an altar is raised, on which reeds are spread, and above which the *ihai* or tablets of those who are no longer alive are hung, in the hope that their spirits will return to visit the places where their earthly life has passed. A rope is stretched across the altar from which various fruits such as millet, water beans, chestnuts and eggplants are hung.

On the 13th, around sunset, an *ogara,* or stalk of wet and dried hemp, is lit; the flame that lasts only for a moment is called *moukai-bi, a* complimentary flame, and its purpose is to welcome the spirits when they arrive. On the evening of the 15th, a new hemp stalk is lit, it is *okouri-bi*, "the farewell flame", the farewell that the living say goodbye to the spirits of their parents, their ancestors.

Series of prints, the number of which is not indicated.

CONTEMPORARY MORALS.

Series of prints, the number of which is not indicated.

THE FORTY-SEVENTH YEAR OLDS.

Second series.

Series of 12 prints.

THE FORTY-SEVEN RONINS.

In this sequel, an impression represents the episode of the costume and weapons supplier, suspected of treason.

Series of prints, the number of which is not indicated.

TWELVE SCENES FROM THE FORTY-SEVEN RONINS.

It is a series of large medallions, containing three heads, treated in a somewhat caricatural manner.

Series of 12 prints.

FAITHFUL WOMEN IN THE HISTORY OF RONINS.

Series of prints, the number of which is not indicated.

THE (immoral) LIFE OF TAIKÔ.

In a board, we see Taïkô, courting a young boy, whose coat of arms on the sleeve clearly indicates his name and family.

Series of prints, the number of which is not indicated.

SCENES FROM JAPANESE LIFE.

This suite is made up of prints representing screens, with, at the bottom, the snaking of the red cord and the display of the large flake knot.

On one of these screens, we see a fish merchant, bare-chested, with a large knife in his hand, cutting a piece of fish, which a woman is waiting for, playing with one of the pins in her hair.

Series of prints, the number of which is not indicated.

THE PLEASURES OF SPRING.

Series of prints, the number of which is not indicated.

THE FIFTY-THREE STATIONS IN TOKAIDO, EACH COMPARED TO A WOMAN'S LIFE.

Suite whose vignette contains, in a circle, a charming little landscape indented by legend, and whose each board represents two honest women, in a bust.

Series that must be 55, with the starting point and the end point, whose complete completion is unknown, but what is very rare in Japanese prints, each with its own number, and it passed through my hands plate 20.

THE BENCHES OF EIGHT FAMOUS PLACES.

In Japan's famous landscapes, the benches are under a kiosk, where tea is served.

Series of prints, the number of which is not indicated.

EIGHT APPOINTMENT VIEWS.

Representations of couples of lovers.

Series of 8 prints.

THE PLEASURES OF THE FOUR SEASONS.

Meeting of two half-body figures.

Series of 4 prints.

THE SIX-NEEDLE FIR TREES.

A group of women half-bodyed, reminiscent of love scenes under the trees.

Series of 6 prints.

TODAY'S BEAUTIFUL WOMEN IN SUMMER SUITS.

A woman in a light dress, peeling a watermelon, a delicacy of the season, that a child has just brought her.

Series of prints, the number of which is not indicated.

THE SEVEN PLEASURES OF SPRING FOR CHILDREN.

Series of 7 prints.

CHILDREN'S GAMES DURING THE FOUR SEASONS.

Series of 4 prints.

CHILDREN PLAYING THE PLAY OF THE FORTY-SEVEN RONINS.

Series of 12 prints.

THE WAY OF DANCING.

One board in this suite depicts a woman holding the strings of a small cart, in front of which a child dances.

Series of prints, the number of which is not indicated.

JEWELRY CHILDREN. *Seven ways to play.*

Series of 7 prints.

PROVERB OF CHILD JEWELRY.

This suite, different from the **CHILDREN'S JEWELRY** suite, contains in the small vignette at the top of the board the story of young Sakala-no-Kintoki and his mother Yama-ouwa.

Series of prints, the number of which is not indicated.

THE SHOOTS OF THE TWO LEAVES. *Children compared to Komaty.*

Series of 7 prints.

CHILDREN PLAYING, COMPARED TO THE SEVEN GODS OF FORTUNE.

Series of 7 prints.

THE CHILDREN DRESSED AS SIX POETS

Series of 6 prints, published in 1790.

EIGHT TENDERNESS. (Mothers and children.)

Series of 8 prints.

MOTHERS AND CHILDREN.

A series of very softly colored prints, in large medallions with a yellow background, enclosed in white sheets, embossed with small striated designs.

Series of prints, the number of which is not indicated.

NEW DESIGNS HAS FIVE DIFFERENT COLORS. (Women with big children.)

This suite takes its name from an imitation of a piece of cloth, placed at the top of the image, which is like a sample of the child's clothing.

Series of 5 prints.

PUPPETS OF THE CHILDREN.

A woman kidnapping a doll above two children, who could be, under her noble hat, the ridiculous representation of a great government figure.

Series of prints, the number of which is not indicated.

PRIDE OF PARENTS IN THE ABILITY OF CHILDREN.

One plate in this suite depicts a mother looking with admiration at her daughter writing poetry on a fan.

Series of prints, the number of which is not indicated.

THE WOMEN CHOSEN. (Ladies of a daimio's court.)

This series has, at the top of each image, a small square containing small everyday objects, the reunion of which could well form a rebus.

Series of prints, the number of which is not indicated.

TWELVE-HOUR OCCUPANCY FOR YOUNG GIRLS. (Honest women.)

Series of 12 prints on a yellow background.

WOMEN'S EDUCATION MODEL.

One of the boards in the suite, which has a green fan as its vignette, depicts a woman in front of a reel, for the manufacture of cotton yarn.

Series of prints, the number of which is not indicated.

TWELVE WOMEN'S JOBS.

Suite of women in bust.

Series of 12 prints.

THE SILKWORM WORKERS.

There is one print, whose clouds at the top of the plate where the Japanese characters of the legends are found, are yellow, and the colorings held almost entirely in the green, yellow and purple colorings, and another print where the shades are pink, and the colorings of a more varied polychromy. There are even differences in the design of women's dresses. Hayashi believes that the yellow draw is the first draw.

A series of 12 prints, making an album or a strip of 12 plates at a time, which can be edited in succession.

THE TWELVE PROFESSIONS.

1. A toothpaste powder saleswoman. - — 2. A writing teacher. - — 3. A painter. - — 4. A silk wadding worker. - — 5. One (wheel binder. - — 6. A balloon maker. - — 7. An embroiderer in silk bas-reliefs, applied on the dresses. - — 8. A seamstress. - — 9. A dry cleaner. - — 10. A *dengaku* maker (to eat). - — 11. A weaver

A series of 11 prints, but which must certainly be twelve, to be complete, a series of an old print, which I only met at Mr. Duret's, a grey print, tinged with a barely colored watercolor.

THE CLOCK OF THE BEAUTIFUL SEX.

Series of 12 prints.

CHARMING COMPETITION.

Women busy with details of their grooming.

Series of prints, the number of which is not indicated.

WOMEN'S TOILET

This sequel to the beginning of Outamaro, to something as heavy as Kiyonaga, without having the power.

Series of prints, the number of which is not indicated.

THE SEVEN DRESS DESIGNS.

Series of 7 prints.

DYEING OF YEDO.

Suite bearing Outamaro's signature, and which may well be from his student Kikumaro.

Series of prints, the number of which is not indicated.

SUMMER DRESSES.

Series of prints, the number of which is not indicated.

CLOTHING OF FIVE DRESSES.

A series of plates, where we see, indeed, on the woman's body, five superposed dresses.

Series of prints, the number of which is not indicated.

NEW BROCADE DESIGNS.

Large women's heads on a yellow background.

A series of prints, the number of which is not indicated, published around 1800.

EIGHT WOMEN COMPARED TO THE EIGHT PHILOSOPHERS.

Series of 8 prints.

COMPARISON OF HEARTS FAITHFULLY LOVING EACH OTHER.

This suite includes all the characters from all the novels and famous love plays.

Many series of prints, the number of which is not indicated.

LOVERS' LOYALTY CONTEST.

Groups of men and women at mid-body level.

Series of 6 prints.

THREE MEETINGS OF TWO PAIRS OF LOVERS.

Series of 8 prints.

THE FIVE LOVERS' PARTIES.

Series of 5 prints.

LOVE POEMS.

A series of large women's heads on an orange background.

Series of prints, the number of which is not indicated.

SIX LOVE POEMS.

One board in this suite depicts a young man taking the breast of a young woman, approached by her mouth, as if he wanted to suckle her, in the bad mood of the infant, who makes an angry hand gesture on his mother's back.

Series of 6 prints.

LOVE DISPUTES WITH this legend: *Clouds in front of the moon.*

The only board I have ever met in this suite represents a horrible old woman, the most dreadful mother-in-law, or mother-in-law, making a scene for the young woman, brutally removing her son by the neck, from her love duo.

Series of prints, the number of which is not indicated.

EIGHT CIRCUMSTANCES OF LIFE COMPARED TO EIGHT PLACES IN JAPAN.

One of the boards depicts a woman tightening her belt with a nervous movement and has the legend: *Storm in the bedroom.*

Series of 8 prints.

THE STORM OF LOVERS.

Groups of several figures in a bust.

Series of prints, the number of which is not indicated.

LOVE SCENES REPRESENTED BY PUPPETS.

Compositions, where the two puppets of the man and the woman, as if placed on the edge of a box, are overhung by the viewers' heads.

A series of prints, the number of which is not indicated, but which would be very large.

FIVE FACES OF BEAUTIFUL WOMEN.

This suite has a magnifying glass at the top of the image.

Series of 5 prints.

THE TEN FACES OF FAMOUS BEAUTIES.

The right print is on a silver background.

Series of 10 prints.

TWELVE FACES OF BEAUTIFUL WOMEN.

Series of 12 prints.

THE ART OF CHOOSING WOMEN. (Courtesans.)

Suite which has as a vignette from the top of the plates signing the series, fragments of split bamboo, by means of which the fortune is drawn there.

Series of 8 prints.

THE CHILDHOOD OF THE GUESHAS.

The gueshas begin by being dancers, then end up becoming singers.

Series of prints, the number of which is not indicated.

THE CHOSEN DANCERS.

A series of large women's heads on a silver background.

A series of impressions, the number of which is not indicated, but at the bottom of each plate is named the dancer represented on it.

Untitled compositions, one of which represents a guesha playing schamisen.

A curious sequence on plain paper and crepe paper, where, in the creamy tone of the background, light cherry blossoms are stripped off, in which the characters of a poem run like insects.

Series of prints, the number of which is not indicated.

A musician, around whose waist a Japanese man lovingly slipped his arm and began to play with his hand the schamisen, which the hand of the female artist had at one point abandoned, to defend herself from the kiss that threatened her.

The only board I met of a suite, whose vignette at the top of the print represents a Chinese man and a Chinese woman playing the same flute.

Series of prints, the number of which is not indicated.

THE FLOWERS OF YEDO. (Singers.)

Set of 7 plates.

ASSORTMENT OF GREAT MODERN COURTESANS.

Continued on a yellow background.

Series of prints, the number of which is not indicated.

THE NEW CHOICE OF SIX FLOWERS. (Women of the Green Houses.)

Series of 6 prints.

TEN DIFFERENT STATES. (Women of the Green Houses.)

Series of 10 prints.

COURTESAN BETWEEN HER TWO KAMOURÔS.

Series signed by Outamaro, in classical writing, with its stamp.

Series of prints, the number of which is not indicated.

COURTESANS.

This series, which has no name, bears as an indicative mark the sign of a Green House, where white characters stand out on a blue background, or, if the background is red, there is always a crest with white characters on a blue background.

Series of prints, the number of which is not indicated.

COURTESANS AND GUESHAS COMPARED TO FLOWERS.

Nothing more graceful in one of these boards than the caressing attitude of two women, one of whom, crouched on the ground, holds and squeezes the wrists of the other in his hands, having his arms passed over his shoulders, in a gentle abandonment of his body leaning over his back, on his neck.

Series of prints, the number of which is not indicated!

COURTESANS COMPARED TO SIX VIEWS OF TAMAGAWA.

Second suite published between 1780 and 1790.

Series of 6 prints.

SIX BEAUTIFUL HEADS OF YEDO, COMPARED TO THE SIX RIVERS OF THE TAMAGAWA RIVER

Courtesans depicted on an embossed white background, the striations of which represent waves. At the top of each woman represented is a small fan, where you can see a view of Tamagawa.

Series of 6 different prints from the first one.

COURTIERS COMPARED TO POETESSES.

Series of 6 prints.

THE SIX KOMATI OF GREEN HOUSES.

First series of portraits of courtesans compared to the poetess.

Series of 6 prints.

THE SEVEN KOMATI OF GREEN HOUSES.

Second suite. Portraits of famous courtesans, whose names are given above each one, and who are called:

Schinowars of Tsuruya.

Kisegawa from Matsubaya.

Tukigama (waterfall).

Wouldn't this Kisegawa from Matsubaya, very often represented by

Outamaro, have been loved by the artist?

Series of 7 prints.

COURTESANS COMPARED TO THE SIX POETS.

Series of 6 prints.

EIGHT WOMEN COMPARED TO EIGHT LANDSCAPES AROUND YOSHIWARA.

Next, where the eight landscapes are represented in the small vignette at the top of the board.

Series of 8 prints.

THE SIX SIGNS OF THE MOST FAMOUS SAKE HOUSES *depicted by six courtesans.*

Series of 6 prints.

FIRST WALK OF THE NEW TOILET.

Series of prints, the number of which is not indicated.

NIWAKA FESTIVAL (CARNIVAL) OF GREEN HOUSES.

Gueshas, some transvestites with the Korean hat on their heads, others wearing a Chinese tiara.

Series of prints, the number of which is not indicated.

THE NIWAKA FESTIVAL.

One of the plates contains the program of the festival, and gives the names of the singers: Kin, Foum, Iyo, Shima.

Series of prints, the number of which is not indicated.

THE NIWAKA FESTIVAL.

A continuation of a smaller format, where in a plate is represented the little Sakata-no-Kin-toki with his mother.

Series of prints, the number of which is not indicated.

BEAUTIFUL WOMEN AT THE NIWAKA FESTIVAL OF THE GREEN HOUSES

Series of prints, the number of which is not indicated.

THE TWELVE HOURS OF GREEN HOUSES.

Series of 12 prints.

THEATRE PERFORMANCES IN GREEN HOUSES.

Series of 10 prints.

COURTESANS IN SHELTERS (during a fire) COMPARED TO EIGHT LOCALITIES.

A series on a yellow background, with a small fan representing the locality.

Series of 8 prints.

Many series of courtesans without titles, but where the plates are named after a courtesan, like these:

Kisegawa (name of a river);

Kana-ôghi (fan of flowers);

Sameyama (colorful mountain);

Hinazuru (stork child).

Courtesans, among whom are still to be found

Kisegawa, the woman who likes to repeat Outamaro's brush.

Original series, where the courtesans are represented in a series of fans presented in height.

Series of prints, the number of which is not indicated.

Nowadays, there are some series made in collaboration with contemporary artists. I will mention, among others, a series executed with Shunyeï, where Outamaro, in each board, represents two women composing the audience, feats of strength performed by Hercules, wrestlers with gargantuan anatomy. In one of these boards we see the tour de force maker standing on one foot, almost horizontally on the ground, his hands turned over and twisted over his back, and picking up, with his mouth, a fan placed on a stool; in another board, it is a second tour maker, who, with his nose attached to his ear by a string, unties him without the help of his hands, by nervous contortions and grimaces of the face.

These small impressions, superior to the *Nishiki-yes* these miraculous impressions, printed on a paper that seems to be elder marrow, in these colors of a melted, harmonized sweetness, that no impression of any people shows us, and with this artistic, amusing, illusioning embossing, and again with, in the middle of the enchanted tones, the introduction so learned, so right, so distinguished, of gold, silver, bronze: these images, as we know, not made for the public, but for the delicate meetings of amateurs and collectors, these images composed in the amusement of tea societies, and forming loose sheets of *books of friends*[59], - these images, of Outamaro, taken by these great color impressions, gave very little of his work and time.

So, we know a relatively small number of sourimonos from Outamaro. However, I would like to point out:

A large sourimono, where we see the legendary ancient couple of Tagasago, implored, on the occasion of great wishes, by the man and woman of Japan, and represented with their lucky attributes: the old

---

[58] The expression sourimono is not absolutely correct, it is rather, as Mr. Gonse says, *drawn in sourimono*: the classical sourimono, the sourimono of Hokusai, Hokkei, Gakutei does not yet exist. Now I don't find that, in these impressions, Outamaro has the originality *of* Gakutei in women, *the* originality of Hokkei in still life.

[59] Mr. Bing notes in a notary that the sourimonos were not exclusively painted for members of tea societies, that very often they surrounded the poems of scholars with whom painters lived in perfect intimacy; they celebrated, in the illustration of a program, the talent of a renowned actor, the talent of a guesha as a musician.

woman with the broom, the old man with this kind of fork - trident, - which is used to collect the needles of the pines.

Another great sourimono representing Tunic known theatrical image that Outamaro drew.

In the small format representations of private life, it is a "New Year's Day Visit", where a Japanese woman fills a visitor's cup with hot sake; a smoking Japanese woman leaning against a small table, and turning her head to the song of a nightingale, perched on a branch of a tree against the house; a courtesan talking with her kamourô; another courtesan walking followed by her two kamourôs.

Of these courtesans with their kamourôs, Mr. Gonse would have five or six little sourimonos.

A funny little smiley face shows us a beast trainer, making a monkey dance, wearing the red cardboard head of the "Lion Dance", in the amazement of a child watching him.

Another little sourimono from the same family is a sourimono where a little girl caresses with a semblance of fear, the articulated head of a tiger-playing toy!

I still have before my eyes a great sourimono, where there are three women: a washerwoman and two courtesans; the washerwoman painted by Tsukmaro, a courtesan by Kunisada, and the courtesan with a silver belt, by Outamaro.

Sourimonos, it must be said, that do not have a personal character, and where nice little women could perfectly be mistaken for Hokusai.

Finally, in the sourimonos that represent objects of private life, in those sourimonos that, for me, are the most perfect sourimonos, and where the reality of small artistic objects for Japanese hands has been rendered in a way that can be said to go beyond industrial artistic success, I will quote just one sourimono:

A bouquet of chrysanthemums of all colors, where white

chrysanthemums stand out in white embossing on the white of the paper, spreading from a vase in sparterie over a half-unrolled kakemono, where you can see a woman, next to the box that contained it.

To these sourimonos, it would be necessary to attach the seven sheets of this album or this complete impossible to find book, of which Mr. Gonse has five plates and Mr. Bing two plates.

Very faded impressions, and sometimes with colors enclosed in two or three tones, sometimes reduced to a chicory green that only tints the landscape.

Here are the five boards owned by Mr. Gonse:

1° Horses grazing freely, in the middle of which a horse rolls on the ground.

2° A smoking line fisherman, while watching three lines.

3° A sennin appearance in the sky, above a woman washing clothes.

4° The fox trap.

3° A daimio sleeping on his horse, driven by a farmer.

These are the two boards owned by Bing:

1° A laundress beating the lighter, to light her pipette.

2° A Japanese lord accompanied by his buffoon.

In this way, Mr. Bing still has some impressions of a brutal *action*, of an action similar to that of Kioto's sourimonos, among which we notice an old man, in the midst of children lying at his feet: an impression imitating a Chinese ink drawing, with a touch of bluish in the stripes of a storm rain.

Another smiley face from Mr. Gonse's collection depicts an old man of the nobility, under a Chinese costume, talking with a warrior, leaning on his spear, in a snow-covered landscape.

Mr. Hayashi believes that this board would be part of *Famous Warriors,* a sequel published from 1775 to 1780, under the influence of

Kiyonaga.

Let us mention again in Mr. Gonse's collection, these pieces printed in sourimonos:

Three children dancing around a lantern.

A beggar showing a sick arm to a woman, whom he seeks to pity.

A tea or beverage merchant of any kind established under a willow tree, in the middle of the countryside.

The greetings of the New Year to the women of a Green House, addressed behind a screen - by the *manzaï,* these joyful dancers in the historical clothes of storks and pine branches: the two emblems of longevity, - and who, on the first Day of the Year, walk the streets, cross the houses, shouting: *manzaï, manzaï ! which* means: *wishes of ten thousand years of life.*

Two long boards, drawn in sourimonos, from Mr. Gillot's collection, one of which represents men measuring a huge tree that they kiss with their outstretched arms; the other represents a peasant woman giving her child to suck on, while an already tall boy throws his line into a river.

These two plates, of a rather rudimentary work, and with figures sometimes treated a little bit in charge, of the series of seven plates, owned by Mr. Gonse and Mr. Bing.

With these two impressions in sourimonos, Mr. Gillot has a board of horses at liberty a little different from that of Mr. Gonse, and where slightly purple, slightly bluish horses, horses related to the horses of Delacroix, engage in a furious galloping, under a sky crossed by a red cloud, made, as on Korin's lacquer boxes, by large lines, broken and interrupted here and there, which makes them look like a series of long dashes.

In Mr. Gillot's work, I still find a series of plates drawn in sourimonos, of an unusual format, - plates that have the elongated shape of kakemonos, and that are not kakemonos.

One of these sourimonos (H 32 c. L 15 c.) represents a fantastic appearance.

On the grey of the night which puts at the top of the sky a very black band, a kind of man-girl, in a white ghostly robe, his long uncultivated hair, swept before him by the wind, brandishes above his head, the anger of a skeleton hand, while from his mouth comes out a zigzagging tongue, like the lock of a whip

The second sourimono (H 39 c. L 17 c.) represents a man with two swords, who seems to be escaping from the hanging up of a hooded woman on his back.

The third sourimono (H 32 c. L15 c.) represents the group of a man and a woman; where the woman supported from behind at the man's shoulder, in a graceful movement, passes her hand over it, to open the umbrella that the man has before him.

These last two sourimonos are of a great style, a sober coloring, a hint of tawny, a hint of beveled, of this coloring of the master's beautiful weather, at the same time as he brought, in the decoration of his dresses, a very recognizable archaism.

EROTIC BOOKS

(Shiingwa.)

BOOKS AND ALBUMS IN COLOR

THE PILLOW POEM: *Outamakura.*

A large color album containing a frontispiece and eleven plates, including a portrait of Outamaro, with a text.

The most beautiful erotic book in Outamaro, published in 1788.

Untitled publication.

Another album, with very tormented poses, with the colors of the impressions of the end of the eighteenth century, and where a woman sees herself, while making love, re hairdressing, her comb between her teeth.

Album composed of nine plates, published without date.

Untitled publication.

A large album in color, on a background slightly tinted grey, where the bodies, of a beautiful large drawing, stand out in their whiteness, in the middle of dresses and fabrics that appear softly watercolored.

In a board a woman, with black hair untied, at her foot, with twisted fingers, thrown into the air and reflected in an ice cream.

An album composed of thirteen plates, published without date.

THE ONES WHO HAVE A LAUGHING HABIT. *Yehon-Waraijôgho.*

The three-volume frontispieces are composed with hands, with tattoos in love with the forearm and wrist, touching natural parts of men or women. A board represents a guesha, at the most serious moment of physical love, playing the schamisen.

Book in color, in three volumes, published without date.

Untitled publication.

A book in color, whose frontispiece is made by a public of phallus in front of a theatre curtain, where a squatting phallus is kneeling, making a pitch, and following this frontispiece two puppet boards, before the erotic compositions.

Book in color, published without date.

THE FLOWERS FALLEN. *Yenipu Hanafubuki.*

Book in color, in three volumes, published in 1802.

BOOKS AND ALBUMS IN BLACK

EVERYONE AWAKE. *Yehon Minamezamé.*

Book printed in black, where the halftones in India ink of the drawing are translated by very delicate stretches of aqua shade, and where fine, fine details appear, as if spared, as well as the microscopic floral details of the dresses.

A first board shows you a woman and a man, whose view of an erotic book blends their mouths, behind the back of the book.

The last board is really a funny and very funny one. A woman and a child look at a distant site, with large glasses, leaning on the edge of a bay overlooking the countryside, and a Japanese man placed nearby, behind the woman, with an eloquent hand indication towards the horizon, tries to draw the child's attention to the beauty of the landscape in the distance, while... and *Japanese* characters*, thrown through the image, make the man say:* - You must be happy with the glasses, they are good, aren't they? *that Japanese characters make the woman say:* - Yes, very good, very good! *make the child say:* - Mom, why do you make so many faces?

The book, published in 1786, and signed by Outamaro in collaboration with Rankokousaï, is curious by the signature, which almost never exists on erotic books.

HAIRSTYLES WITH A JADE COMB. *Yehon Tamatus-highè.*
Book in black, much more carefully printed than the erotic ones published later, published in 1789.

THE TREASURE STORE. *Takara-ghura.*
Book in black, in three volumes, published without date.

SECRET LETTER OF THE NIGHT. *Yèhon-Yomizu-fumi.*
Book in black, in three volumes, published without date.

A THOUSAND KINDS OF COLORS. *Tigusa-no-iro.*
Book in black published in three volumes, undated.

THE SECRET MIRROR. *Yehon Masukaghami.*
Book in black, in three volumes, published without date.

A THOUSAND COMPLAINTS OF LOVE. *Yehon Ironotikusa.*
Book in black, in three volumes, published without date.

TSUKUMA'S POT. *Tsumanabe.*

Book in black, in three volumes, published without date.

FIRST ESSAY ON WOMEN. *Yehon Hime-hajinré.*

Frontispieces made with geese, swans, crows.

Book in black, in three volumes, published without date.

POSTFACE

I open W. de Seidlitz's big book, *Japanese woodblock,* and
immediately, in the preface, I find this sentence:

The first essay on Japanese engraving, Anderson's
monograph: *Japanese Wood Engraving,* appeared in 1895 in the
Portfolio. The first attempt at the history of this art was
Strange's *Japanese illustration in* 1897....

However, *the Outamaro* de Concourt is from 1891, and W.
de Seidlitz acknowledges the importance of this book when
he writes:

... Where I found myself faced with a "better prepared"
subject, such as for example for Outamaro and Hokusai,
already studied in depth by Goncourt, I was naturally able
to be more complete. "We see by this which authority
Edmond de Goncourt had as a Japanese collector... We
should therefore not be surprised by his preface, his claim:

It has been so interesting to make the intimate story of
women and things of the eighteenth century, almost as much
as anyone else, that my taste for the new, the undeflowered,
leads me, as old as I am, to try, for the human century I love,
and who is human among the peoples of both hemispheres, to
attempt the history of Japanese art, under more or less the
same conditions of virginity of the documents in which I
wrote the *moral* and artistic history of the *Eighteenth Century*
and the Revolution in France.

Moreover, my great friend, Theodore Duret, in *Books and
Illustrated Albums of Japan,* telling us about his discoveries and

those of Cernuschi, during a study trip from which they brought back (1871-1872) the art bronzes that can be seen at the Monceau Park Museum and illustrated books by Hokousaï or his contemporaries[60], expressly tells us that Goncourt already had a collection of Japanese books.

This is all the more surprising since curiosity, at that time, preferred bronzes and porcelains, and that it was necessary to be a true artist oneself to discover the beauty in these engravings so far from our European art. In this regard, I quote Duret, the book mentioned above:

The first traveler, M. de Chassiron, who, in a story published in 1861, had given some reproductions of Japanese engravings taken from Hokusai's work, did not imagine seeing works of art there; he reproduced them in his book under the title : *Natural history, caricatures, country customs, and,* moreover, this reproduction had gone unnoticed. »

It was at the time of the publication of *Outamaro* that I met Goncourt... I went through the Japanese albums with him, and it was an initiation for me, because I was living, with most of my contemporaries, on some elementary ideas about Japanese artists. I was particularly dazzled by the splendor of Outamaro. These sumptuous boards struck my imagination: I knew that Outamaro was for me a brother in spirit by his love of the woman he so voluptuously wrapped in the great Japanese fabrics, in folds, contours, falls and dress colors so beautiful that the heart fails to look at them, to imagine what they represent of exquisite research and

---

[60] Later donated by Duret to the National Library.

enjoyment. For the exterior of women's clothing denounces a people's conception of love, and this love is itself only a form of higher thought crystallized around a source of joy... Outamaro, painter of Japanese love, will die of this love; because we must not forget that Japanese love is mostly erotic. The great artist's *shungwa* show *the other side* of the man's concerns, whose delicious images of women fill hundreds of books and albums, and, undoubtedly, it would be worth showing the countless affinities of art with eroticism... If the *Outamaro* maste, the painter Sekiyen, could say of the magnificent book of Insects:

Here are the first works made with the "heart", it is that Outamaro's heart appears in the search for the beauty of animals with this effusion that we will find later when he describes the women of *Yoshiwara*. I would not easily believe in the love of beauty in an artist who is not a sensual one. It is obvious that nature wanted to make procreation benefit from all sentimental acquisitions, or, if we prefer, that it is sex that is at, the basis of aesthetic sensations and that develops by grouping them together, in the same way that nature acts when it puts the child in the form of schemas in creative cells; it thus becomes our best sense to externalize the art of which we have said a lot by affirming that it exists mainly by schematization, by stylization....

Outamaro therefore belongs to the immense legion of erotic artists. Japan offers him a resource that the rudeness of European public love would have denied him: the *Yoshiwara* has nothing in common with our brothels; it was, especially in the eighteenth century, a garden of delights; it was a refined court for kind prostitutes, versed in letters and rites of the most exquisite politeness. Eros taking the figure of love, Outamaro had no difficulty in gathering all the elements of his work in "green houses" of which he became the official painter.

Edmond de Goncourt masterfully exposes the history of Japanese art from the *Buddhist School* to the *School of Life*, including *the Tosa School* and the *Kano School*. I could add details that have been better known since then; but I will only point out the extreme continuity of Japanese art. Nothing can give a better idea of this than the representation of faces, especially the woman's face. Since the earliest antiquity, we have found this mask motionless, elongated, reduced to elementary lines, always the same, following a gun from China... The painters will succeed the painters for a thousand years, and this conventional mask will remain the face of the woman... I am convinced that this is not a special modality in Japanese art. Let us only recall the slow evolution of Egyptian art, the persistence of *cannons,* the hieratic poses, fixed once and for all, and the diversity of the gods alone creating the diversity of types...

Will we dare to claim that the Assyrian, Egyptian sculptors, that the Japanese painters were unable to grasp the nuances of life, those that Hokusai finally reproduced with such brilliant prodigality? That would be irony. To suppose that an Outamaro, a Toyokouni, a Kiyonaga were incapable of correcting some childish errors of perspective; to suppose that they could not have broken with the tradition of this Chinese face, with the convention of attitudes, with the biases taken of decoration; to suppose that these great artists remained faithful to customs, such as not to put shadows or reflections, only because their eyes could not perceive these shadows and reflections, wouldn't it be so much, absurd suppositions? What was stopping them? They respected a prescription that was undoubtedly tacit; being aware that this obedience to a higher discipline deprived art of its individual character, making it a specific function.

Excessive individualization thus appears to be the cause of the evils from which our Western art suffers. A great artist will perform beautiful works, whatever the forms imposed on him. The mediocre artist, on the contrary, will be stopped by the frames of a secular art like a fish by a net....

Shouldn't we remember that Manet has always defended himself from being a "window smasher"? The Olympia, so disparaged in an era of romantic decadence, does it not offer all the characteristics of great classical works, does it not resemble Titian, Velasquez? The definitive choice of the Olympia's almost hieratic pose corroborates this point of view: the sketch communicated by Duret in his book on Manet shows that the painter let himself be tempted by a bad taste then all-powerful, and that he tried the freer and more banal attitudes with which the mediocre painters flatter the passions of a crowd that one must never admit to the honor of judging... Similarly, we will better understand Monet's effort by starting from these first paintings where he proves his perfect possession of the *transmitted craft...*

Instead of throwing themselves into an anarchic freedom and thus impoverishing art by substituting a purely individual work for the work of the species, instead of being satisfied with a *leg* or a *technique, with a* weak and ineffective personal vision, our young men must strongly attach themselves to

Western art as it was taught to them by their father; they must study it, create structures that will always overflow them as society overflows the individual; then, having acquired "control", annex themselves with new forms, new ways, new ideas... One of those whom our poor art libertarians readily cite as an example, Paul Cézanne, told Geffroy:

I like Baron Gros; how can I "take these jokes seriously"?

"These jokes" were the innovators anyway. Outamaro humbly received the tradition that came to him from the great Kiyonaga, from the kind and ingenious Harunobou, and that was taught to him by masters such as Sekiyen and Shunsho. Goncourt notes that he became a kind of aristocrat of painting, disdaining to paint theater people, or even simply men. The women alone occupied him, filled his art. He settled with his publisher at the entrance to the Yoshiwara and soon became the wonderful artist we know...

He is accused of having been one of the most eager zealots to spread the fashion of the long figure among women, the fashion to give these figures incredible proportions. He followed, forced this fashion, but, wrong in proportions, his great heads remained works of wonderful art. We find this particularity in Rodin.... An almost classic sculptor, in love with antiquity, after he had acquired mastery, he went through a period of trial and error, of acute research where we can, with the compass in hand, demonstrate that he was going beyond the rules of anatomy. He hardly cared, knowing full well, at the bottom of his genius, that if he broke the molds, he was in possession of making them again, more beautiful in their novelty. Let us never confuse the effort of a giant artist in struggle against banality, making a clean slate of the skill, grace and charm that surround him, holding him prisoner of old formulas, even if it means returning to tradition with new forces; let us never confuse this effort with that of young ephebes, just out of the diapers, who would like to impose themselves by an ignorant and powerless eccentricity...

Art shows a terrible tendency to become popular in the hands of the seductive mediocre... In our countries, there are many men who can hold a chisel, a brush, a feather... Rodin's Balzac then becomes an answer to the question asked by an idolatrous audience, knowing only how to choose among so many works that it considers perfect in their banality.

"What to learn to see? ", asks Rodin... Here are the laws of sculpture: I force them in order to make them more visible... Light and shadows make such and such a thing of a face: beauty is an original design and not the more or less similar reproduction of a physiognomy.

What a lesson for us, if we knew how to take advantage of it, to find in the Japanese, in a civilization with no connection to ours, the same crises, the same laws of development!

Many people wonder what was the cause of Japanese decadence ...

Art stops at the political revolution of 1868, which will throw Japan into the world community of peoples. It stops without decadence. The last names mentioned by historians are those of Shunsen, Kunisada, Hokusai, Hiroshige. This one goes until 1858, and he dies of cholera in full force...

Unparalleled flowering! Hokusai, despite the resistance that the Germans want to put into it, is the greatest of all Japanese artists; in him is concentrated, combined, summarized a thousand years of prodigious efforts. Hiroshige is a marvel.

Should we believe that this development could have continued? It would be foolhardy to rule on this point; but, in any case, it was as if the Japanese nation had lived just long enough from its old life to give birth to the extraordinary man we all admire today. The curtain can fall on Hokusai: the Japanese play is played! To finish a colossal work, life was granted to him until he was 89 years old... He was not tired; he hoped to live a century!

If I had to look for, however, the master who could act as an intermediary between yesterday's and tomorrow's Japanese art, I would point out Hiroshigué, reminding me with emotion of his landscapes and his animals.

In the eyes of his contemporaries, Hokusai seemed to be the innovator of innovators:

"Hokusai, known as Hirata in 1818, is incomparable;" while all his predecessors were more or less slaves to classical traditions and acquired rules, he alone emancipated his brush and drew according to the inspirations of his heart. Whatever his eyes, devoted to nature, absorb in them, he renders it with truth and precision. »

There is much to be said against such an opinion. I have before me one of the most beautiful landscapes of Fousyama, the one that shows the peak on the other side of the Sumida: Hokusai probably returned it as he saw it, but he saw it with Nippon eyes, without shadows, without reflections. This proves that he saw things through the painting of the six centuries preceding his own. Let us learn not to be ungrateful and recognize what Hugo owes Racine.

Outamaro is the Japanese Racine. I don't pretend to invent this parallel; just as we find a lot of people in our country who still prefer the great classic to the great romantic, I would understand that there are Japanese to put Outamaro above Hokusai....

Kiyonaga abdicated like Charles V. Died in 1815, he stopped working in 1801, after a long period of almost complete abandonment from 1793 to 1801. He ended up in glory, and his time certainly did not believe that he would be outdated.

It was, however, by Outamaro. And God knows that, in this fruitful period, he had rivals worthy of the highest rank, especially Yeishi, a descendant like him of the Kano school, that is, the Chinese school, and Toyokouni, son of a Buddhist image sculptor from Yedo. To be able to take the lead over such men, what prestige had to be used by the painter of the Green Houses! He certainly surpassed Yeishi by the ardor of his production and the variety of his work; but Yeishi has such a wonderful style and refined elegance that many of his productions remain unparalleled...

An observation that resembles Outamaro with Raphael is that of their early death.... They were both probably of poor health, although Outamaro's premature death is generally attributed to the odious prison sentence he received for political reasons... But he has the character of the great young dead men, the privilege of Pascal, that of Racine, that of Raphael; all dazzle their contemporaries with surprising gifts... Hokusai is rather similar to Michelangelo; it develops slowly. During the lifetime of Yeishi and Outamaro, it was only secondary; it did not reach their grace, elegance or morbidity. The Japanese, who value nobility more in great beauty than observation and spirit, placed Hokusai below Outamaro. Europeans do not ratify this ranking. For me, I think that Japan was not wrong to believe that caricature, however great its qualities may be, offers more grip on the trompe-l'oeil, surprises by a complexity of attitudes more apparent than real, and, finally, makes it possible to take with the truth unwelcome licenses to men of taste. In the theatre, the strong roles, the comedians are, in short, easier to play than the serious or heroic roles... No one can blame the comedian for a forced trait, as long as it makes people laugh; and, as long as gestures and expressions are distorted to make them characteristic, this distortion does not obey the so rigorous laws of beauty, which is destroyed by the slightest deviation...

Today we have an unfortunate tendency to confuse realism with coarseness, mind with jest, originality with exaggeration; let us reread, look at our masters, and take a more accurate idea of all these things by studying Outamaro's magnificent work.

J.-H. ROSNY young, from the Académie Concourt.

N. D. E.

The first edition of this book was published in 1891 by Charpentier, in Paris, in a volume in-12.

TABLE OF CONTENTS

Biography of Outamaro